"Reading this wonderful book resembles exploring a spiritual treasure trove. You encounter one sparkling insight after another regarding God's marvelous grace. In accessible prose Timothy George helps us to understand better just how amazing God's sovereign grace actually is. The book's message will instruct, encourage, and refresh your Christian life. After all, God's sovereign grace is a worthy subject for our daily reflection and most profound meditation."

John D. Woodbridge, Research Professor of Church History and Christian Thought, Trinity Evangelical Divinity School

"*Amazing Grace* by Timothy George is an amazing little book! It is biblical and practical, theological and missional. It delves into the mystery of divine sovereignty and human responsibility, providing wonderful insight while also allowing the tensions of Scripture to remain. I was blessed by the book the first time I read it. I enjoyed this edition even more."

Danny Akin, President, Southeastern Baptist Theological Seminary

"*Amazing Grace* is a gracious and graceful defense of the doctrines of grace. Although this book began its life as a piece dedicated to helping Southern Baptists understand the dispute between Calvinists and non-Calvinists in their denomination, it should help anyone appreciate why the apprehension of God's grace must be absolutely central to Christian life and worship. May many, by God's grace, read it and adopt its wise and irenic posture in the various controversies that a biblically faithf   "

Mark  Philosophy, ton College

"It is hard to be simultaneously boring and polarizing, but the Calvinism/ Arminianism debates typically are both. The arguments are often filled with the kind of 'bitter jealousy' and 'selfish ambition,' the Scriptures identify as 'demonic.' Timothy George's *Amazing Grace* is different. In this book, a world-renowned Christian scholar walks through the biblical texts about God's purpose of grace in a way that is honest, easy to understand, and charitable to those who disagree. Whether you are a Calvinist, an Arminian, or somewhere in between, you'll learn something from this book. You'll also see modeled how to converse with those who disagree with you. And, more than all that, you'll put the book down at the end and worship our love-driven, grace-filled God. This is the best book on God's grace in print today."

Russell D. Moore, Dean,
The Southern Baptist Theological Seminary

"Biblically faithful, historically well informed, and irenic in tone, this wise work from the pen of Timothy George is a sure guide for anyone perplexed about questions of divine sovereignty, grace, and human responsibility. Highly recommended!"

Graham A. Cole, Professor of Biblical and Systematic Theology,
Trinity Evangelical Divinity School

"George has given us a biblically based and theologically formed treatment of the amazing grace of God in the salvation of men and women. Historically informed, timely in its application, and gracious in spirit, this lucid and readable work will be beneficial for many, especially those who struggle with the tensions involved in God's initiative in our salvation and our response to God's abounding grace for sinners. I am pleased to recommend this insightful treatment of this important theme, which will be particularly helpful to pastors, church leaders, and church study groups."

David S. Dockery, President, Union University

AMAZING
GRACE

AMAZING GRACE

GRACE

{ *God's Pursuit, Our Response* }

SECOND EDITION

TIMOTHY GEORGE

CROSSWAY

WHEATON, ILLINOIS

Amazing Grace: God's Pursuit, Our Response, Second Edition
Copyright © 2000, 2011 by Timothy George
Published by Crossway
        1300 Crescent Street
        Wheaton, Illinois 60187

First edition 2000
First printing, Second Edition 2011
Cover design: Amy Bristow
Printed in the United States of America

Unless otherwise indicated, Scripture quotations are from the ESV® Bible (*The Holy Bible, English Standard Version®*), copyright © 2001 by Crossway. Used by permission. All rights reserved.

Scripture quotations marked KJV are from the King James Version of the Bible.

Scripture quotations marked MESSAGE are from *The Message*. Copyright © by Eugene H. Peterson 1993, 1994, 1995, 1996, 2000, 2001, 2002. Used by permission of NavPress Publishing Group.

Scripture references marked NEB are from *The New English Bible* © The Delegates of the Oxford University Press and The Syndics of the Cambridge University Press, 1961, 1970.

Scripture quotations marked NIV are from the *Holy Bible, New International Version®*. Copyright © 1973, 1978, 1984 Biblica. Used by permission of Zondervan. All rights reserved. The "NIV" and "New International Version" trademarks are registered in the United States Patent and Trademark Office by Biblica. Use of either trademark requires the permission of Biblica.

Scripture references marked NKJV are from *The New King James Version*. Copyright © 1982, Thomas Nelson, Inc. Used by permission.

Scripture references marked PHILLIPS are from *The New Testament in Modern English*, translated by J. B. Phillips © 1972 by J. B. Phillips. Published by Macmillan.

All emphases in Scripture quotations have been added by the author.

Trade paperback ISBN: 978-1-4335-1548-4
PDF ISBN: 978-1-4335-1549-1
Mobipocket ISBN: 978-1-4335-1550-7
ePub ISBN: 978-1-4335-2477-6

Library of Congress Cataloging-in-Publication Data
George, Timothy.
Amazing grace : God's pursuit, our response / Timothy George. —2nd ed.
    p. cm.
  Includes bibliographical references and index.
  ISBN 978-1-4335-1548-4 (tp)
    1. Grace (Theology). 2. Theological anthropology—Christianity. 3. Christian life. 4. Baptists—Doctrines. I. Title.
BT761.3.G46 2011
234—dc22
                                                         2010039161

Crossway is a publishing ministry of Good News Publishers.

VP		22	21	20	19	18	17	16	15	14	13	12	11
14	13	12	11	10	9	8	7	6	5	4	3	2	1

For

Lee Atlas
Barbara Bruce
Mark Dever
Mark and Jackie DeVine
Barry Harvey
Paul House
Annemarie Kidder
Timothy McCoy
Al Mohler
Elizabeth Newman
Hal and Mary Anne Poe
Thom Rainer
Zechariah Schariah
Michael Spencer (1956–2010)

They taught a young professor how to teach
and still encourage him to learn.

CONTENTS

PREFACE

For it is by grace you have been saved, through faith—and this
not from yourselves, it is the gift of God—not by works,
so that no one can boast. ~ EPHESIANS 2:8–9

Amazing Grace was published in its first edition ten years ago as the 2001 Doctrine Study for the Southern Baptist Convention. At that time there was growing concern, even alarm in some quarters, over what was called the "Calvinism controversy" within America's largest Protestant denomination. It was felt that a clear, simple exposition of what are known as the doctrines of grace might shed more light than heat on this growing dispute, and I was asked to write this book with that purpose in mind. In fact, over the past decade many thousands of believers, churches, and associations within the Baptist world and beyond have found this little book to be helpful in just that way. In response to many requests from pastors and church leaders for a new edition, *Amazing Grace* is being published again, with only slight changes, in hopes that it will continue to serve something of its original purpose.

One of the changes is in the subtitle. "God's Initiative—Our Response" has become "God's Pursuit—Our Response." What's the difference between an initiative and a pursuit? *Initiative* is from the

Latin word *initia*, which means "beginning." An initiative is the act of taking the first step of originating or beginning something new. The Bible says it is God who always takes the initiative in the salvation of human beings. It is God who creates, originates, and regenerates. This is what was meant in the first subtitle, "God's Initiative—Our Response." But *pursuit* is a stronger, more action-oriented word. Jesus said that he had been sent "to seek and to save the lost" (Luke 19:10). In the Old Testament, Jonah tried to run away from God but the Lord pursued him, sought him, and finally found him under the castor-oil plant in Nineveh. The second part of the subtitle is also important for there is a genuine human response to the God who seeks and saves. The apostolic presentation of the gospel always included a twofold imperative: repent and believe. The pursuit of grace leads to a vital relationship with the living Lord for, as the Westminster Shorter Catechism says (Q. 1), the chief end of man is to glorify God and to enjoy him forever.

The title of this book is the name of the best-known and most-beloved hymn of the Christian faith. "Amazing Grace" was written by John Newton, a former slave trader whose life was rescued from ruin by the surprising grace of God, which came to him "through many dangers, toils, and snares." Newton became an Anglican minister in the village of Olney and later served a large church in London. There Newton befriended the Baptist shoemaker-pastor William Carey, who became "the father of modern missions" by carrying the gospel of grace to faraway India. Grace is the great theme of the Bible from first to last. *Sola gratia*, "by grace alone," is the most fundamental affirmation of the Reformation and of all true evangelical Christianity. Thus, the central theme of this book applies to believers of all denominations even though some of the examples and illustrations are drawn from the Baptist family of faith.

John Bunyan's masterpiece of the spiritual life, *The Pilgrim's Progress*, tells the story of a man who sets out from home carrying a great burden. Someone named Evangelist points him toward a celestial city shining in the distance. Along the way, the man loses his burden, and, though there are many struggles and battles yet to come, he is sustained through them all by the illimitable love of God. The burden in the story is sin. The city of light is heaven. Before he leaves home, the man's name is Graceless. When his burden is lifted, his name becomes Christian. Christian's story is our story too. We are saved by grace alone, through faith alone, in Jesus Christ alone. And in that same grace we walk, step-by-step, toward "the city that has foundations, whose designer and builder is God" (Heb. 11:10).

As wonderful as grace is, it has provoked some of the most heated controversies in the history of the Christian church. In this study, we shall look at some of these debated questions while never losing sight, I trust, of the reality we are discussing: God's free and sovereign favor to ill-deserving sinners. God's great ocean of truth is much deeper than our finite minds can fathom. I am keenly aware that there is much more to be said about grace than I am able to say in this brief study. My purpose throughout is more devotional than academic: God's grace should provoke wonder and worship among all God's children. This study is an exercise in theology in the sense that the great Puritan divine William Ames defined it—the knowledge of living in the presence of the living God.

My own personal apprehension of God's pursuing love and sovereign grace did not come in a sudden flash of insight. It has evolved over a long period of struggle, questioning, and arguing with God. Like the apostle Paul, I do not consider myself to have arrived at a perfect understanding of the many questions and issues posed in this book. I am still learning. I still "press on to make it my own, because Christ Jesus has made me his own" (Phil. 3:12). There is no place for arrogance or one-upmanship in the Christian life and especially in the Calvinist life. Of all people, Calvinists should know that whatever understanding we have obtained into the mystery of divine grace, we have received it the same way we have received salvation itself—as a sheer gift (1 Cor. 4:7). This means that we should be patient and gentle with our brothers and sisters in Christ who are where we once were in our journey toward a fuller understanding.

I once participated in a theological seminar at Cambridge University. One of the speakers had given a paper that was simply terrible, and there had been several brutal exchanges in the discussion that followed. When we retired for tea, several of us were quite upset by what we had heard from this speaker and his unyieldedness in defending what seemed to us a very misguided point of view. One of us turned to Dr. Ronald Wallace, a great Scottish theologian, and asked with some exasperation, "What shall we say now? What are we going to do?" With great wisdom, Professor Wallace replied, "Young men, you must pray, 'O Lord, open his eyes that he may see.'" At the end of the day, it is not our brilliant arguments, nor our great learning or quick wit that can bring anyone to believe in the doctrines of grace. It is the Lord who must open all of our eyes.

One

OUR GRACIOUS GOD

Great God of wonders! All thy ways
Are worthy of thyself—divine:
And the bright glories of thy grace
Among thine other wonders shine;
Who is a pardoning God like thee?
Or who has grace so rich and free?

~ SAMUEL DAVIES

If you were asked to sum up the entire message of the Bible in just one word, which word would you choose? *Reconciliation, salvation, justification, atonement, faith, love, eternal life?* All of these are wonderful words, but the word I would choose is *grace.* The very last verse in the Bible summarizes the message of Holy Scripture from Genesis to Revelation: "The grace of the Lord Jesus be with all" (Rev. 22:21).

The word *grace* is found some 150 times in the New Testament alone. A quick look in any Bible concordance will show how *grace* is used to describe the most basic truths of the Christian faith. The God of the Bible is preeminently the God of grace (1 Pet. 5:10). Jesus came into the world "full of grace and truth" (John 1:14). The Holy

Spirit is the Spirit of grace (Zech. 12:10). God's throne is a throne of grace (Heb. 4:16). We receive forgiveness according to the riches of divine grace (Eph. 1:7). We are chosen, justified, and sanctified, and one day will be glorified all because of grace. Every Christian is called to be a good steward of the manifold grace of God (1 Pet. 4:10). God's grace brings salvation (Titus 2:11). The good news we proclaim is the gospel of grace, and if anyone preaches a different gospel, Paul does not hesitate to say, in the boldest language imaginable, that he should go straight to hell! Yes, as harsh as it sounds, this is what the Greek phrase *anathema estō* in Galatians 1:9 means: "Let him be accursed," that is, eternally condemned by God!

Grace is the great theme of the Bible, and it is also present in every act of Christian worship and devotion. We say "grace" at the table before we eat our meals. Christian baptism celebrates the triumph of God's grace in bringing a lost man or woman out of the darkness of sin into the marvelous light of new life in Christ. In the Lord's Supper we remember God's gracious favor in sending Christ to be our Redeemer, even as we commune with him through the power of the Holy Spirit and look forward to the marriage supper of the Lamb, when by God's grace we shall see the Savior face-to-face. Frequently our worship services are closed by a benediction extolling the triune God of grace and love: "The grace of the Lord Jesus Christ and the love of God and the fellowship of the Holy Spirit be with you all" (2 Cor. 13:14).

And, oh, how Christians love to sing about God's grace!

Marvelous, infinite, matchless grace,
Freely bestowed on all who believe![1]

When I was a teenager I often listened to a radio broadcast called *Revival Time* with Assemblies of God evangelist C. M. Ward. At the end of every program, as Dr. Ward gave the gospel invitation, the choir sang,

The cross upon which Jesus died
Is a shelter in which we can hide;
And its grace so free is sufficient for me,
And deep is its fountain as wide as the sea.

There's room at the cross for you. . . .[2]

But no hymn is more beloved than John Newton's "Amazing Grace! How Sweet the Sound." The son of a British shipmaster, Newton entered naval service himself and became a slave trader. Amid the perils of the sea, he was rescued from a life of despair and debauchery. Newton later became, along with William Wilberforce, a major force in the abolition of the slave trade. In looking back on his life and the transformation that had occurred, he could account for this change only by appealing to the grace of God. And so he wrote:

Amazing Grace! How sweet the sound,
That saved a wretch like me!
I once was lost, but now am found,
Was blind, but now I see.

On any Sunday you can still hear it sung in great cathedrals and in small country churches, on the radio and television and YouTube, by gospel quartets and rock artists and operatic soloists, in hundreds of languages around the world:

'Twas grace that taught my heart to fear,
And grace my fears relieved;
How precious did that grace appear
The hour I first believed![3]

There is a sense in which God's grace is so simple that even a small child can grasp its meaning. And yet it is so profound that the most learned theologians cannot fully comprehend its wonder and beauty and power. For grace is not only amazing; it is also perplexing. When we think about it, and God does want us to think about it (see 2 Tim. 2:15; 1 Pet. 3:15), the doctrine of grace raises many questions in our minds. From what source comes God's grace? If it is true that humans can do nothing to save themselves, why are there so many commands and exhortations in the Bible? What about predestination? How does God's sovereignty relate to human responsibility? Is the invitation to believe in Christ really meant for everyone or just the elected few, the "frozen chosen"? What about falling from grace? Is it possible to lose our salvation by falling into sin? Does God really know everything that will happen before it occurs? If God is sovereign, why do suffering and evil exist in the world? How should we understand the grace of God in relation to missions and evangelism? Why are election or predestination sometimes sources of division, even among Bible-believing Christians?

These are some of the questions we are going to deal with in this study. But I want to make clear right from the start that I do not claim to have completely satisfactory answers to all these questions. The apostle Paul had personal revelations and visitations to heaven not available to most ordinary Christians. But even he was forced to admit that "we know in part and we prophesy in part. . . . For now we see in a mirror dimly" (1 Cor. 13:9, 12).

The study of God's grace is like staring into the sun on a bright cloudless day. That is a dangerous thing to do. Our eyes can be damaged, even blinded, by such unobstructed vision. Yet only by means of the sun can we see anything at all—the blue sky, beautiful flowers, mountains, meadows, all of God's multicolored creation. Only a stupid person would decide to live his whole life inside a bunker beneath the ground for fear of walking outside in the sunshine. And so with God's grace, we must not peer too directly into matters God has not revealed so clearly, lest our spiritual vision be blurred. But we must never forget that only by God's grace can we see anything at all. May God—a God who is far greater than our best ideas and infinitely more marvelous than our finest theologies—help us to approach this subject with reverence, humility, and a sense of wonder.

I recognize that not everyone will agree with even the provisional answers I shall offer on some of these disputed matters. Thus in the interest of full disclosure, let me say up front that I write from the perspective of a Reformed Baptist theologian. This view, I believe, represents the mainstream of historic Baptist theology through the centuries. My views on God's grace do not differ from those held by such evangelically committed and missionary-minded Baptist leaders as John Bunyan, Roger Williams, William Carey, Andrew Fuller, Luther Rice, Adoniram Judson, and Charles Haddon Spurgeon.

In fairness, though, it needs to be said that there has always been within the Baptist tradition a variety of views on how God's grace should be understood, on the proper balance between divine sovereignty and human responsibility. Throughout this study, I shall note areas of significant divergence while disclosing my own views as well. Evangelical Christians committed to historic Christian orthodoxy, whether Calvinists or Arminians, share more in common about the doctrine of grace than their disputes and battles have sometimes shown. I want to emphasize this common ground, for it is liable to be blurred by zealous combatants on both sides. At the same time, I want to encourage all of us to a deeper searching of God's Word on this crucial doctrine. Tertullian indicated that the Christians of ancient Carthage had a certain reputation among the pagans of that city: "See," they said, "how they love one another!"[4] When the world looks at the church today, what they need most to see are not Christians carrying on graceless debates about the doctrine of grace. What the world needs to see are believers who have been transformed by grace, who love one another, and who are reaching out to a lost world in Jesus' name.

In recent years, there has been a lively discussion of these issues among many Baptists, and I think this is a good thing. In some measure, this discussion has been prompted by a return to a sounder doctrine of biblical authority. If the Bible really is the Word of God, inerrant and infallible in all that it claims, then it becomes very important to determine exactly what the Bible does teach about such important matters as God's grace and our response to it. While Baptists may not agree on every aspect of interpretation, at the end of the day we will submit our judgment to the final bar of Holy Scripture. We are grateful for Baptist heroes of the past, and we may rightly turn to them for guidance. But W. T. Conner, E. Y. Mullins, Augustus H. Strong, Charles H. Spurgeon, John A. Broadus, James P. Boyce, and other Baptist theologians whose works we can read with much profit may all be quite wrong on this or that matter of doctrine. From first to last, our warrant is God's Word written! Like the disciples of Berea, we must examine the Scriptures to see whether these things are true (Acts 17:11). Like Martin Luther at the Diet of Worms, may our consciences remain ever captive to the Holy Scriptures.

WHAT GRACE IS

There are many definitions of *grace*, but one of my favorites is the one I first learned as a little boy in Sunday school: grace is "God's Riches At Christ's Expense." We must not stumble over the simplicity of that phrase lest we also miss its profundity. It points to three elements that are essential in a biblical understanding of grace.

First, grace originates with God. God initiates grace. As Paul says in Romans 9:16, "So then it depends not on human will or exertion, but on God, who has mercy." If any creature has any claim on grace whatsoever, it is solely because that grace has been given, bestowed, freely and undeservedly granted by God.

Second, God's grace is inexhaustible, irrepressible, overflowing. God is not stingy. He is "rich in mercy," Paul says (Eph. 2:4). Once a violent persecutor of God's people, a converted Paul declared, "The grace of our Lord overflowed for me" (1 Tim. 1:14). When John Bunyan wrote his own spiritual autobiography, he picked up on this same theme, calling it *Grace Abounding to the Chief of Sinners* (see Rom. 5:20). One of the problems with the term *limited atonement* (a phrase we shall come back to in chapter 4) is that it suggests that something is missing or lacking in God's grace. Like cold drinks at a picnic, the supply is said to be "limited" for fear that it might run out, that there might not be enough to go around! But this could not possibly be true of God's grace, for it is infinite and knows no such bounds.

Finally, grace is God's riches *at Christ's expense*. We should never think of grace apart from Jesus Christ. Jesus is the incarnate Son of God, the embodiment of divine grace. It is "from the fullness of his grace" that we have received blessing upon blessing (John 1:16, NIV). This means that while grace is radically free, it is never cheap, for it cost God the dearest thing he had, the sacrifice of his Son.

In chapter 3 we shall take up the theme of God's sovereignty in salvation, but it is equally important to stress the sovereign freedom of God in creation as well. We cannot understand grace at all without considering this question: Who is God and why did he make the world in the first place? Some people teach that God made the world because, way back in the vast reaches of eternity past, he had somehow grown lonely. He created the world, so this theory goes, in order to have something to love. What an utterly pagan notion of God! It supposes that in his innermost being, God lives utterly alone—a monad, superior and transcendent to be sure, but isolated and aloof in his omnipotence. Arius, a false teacher of the fourth century, believed this. He wrote, "We know there is one God, *alone* unbegotten, *alone* eternal, *alone* without beginning, *alone* true, *alone* immortal. . . ."[5]

The Bible gives us a very different picture of God. Here we learn that within the being of God himself lies a mysterious living love, a dynamic reciprocity of surrender and affirmation, of giving and receiving, among the Father, the Son, and the Holy Spirit. God is not the Alone with the Alone. The Maker of heaven and earth is both one and tripersonal. He is the triune God of holiness and love.

God does not express his ultimate reality in terms of brute power and force alone. This is not the most decisive mark of God's divinity. The relationship of total and mutual self-giving, by which the Father gives everything to the Son, and the Son offers back all that he has to glorify the Father, is what makes God really God. The love of the Father and the Son for one another is established and sealed by the Holy Spirit, who proceeds from both.

If all this is true, then why on earth did God make the world in the first place? Not because he had to, but simply because he chose to, for his "good pleasure," as Paul puts it (Eph. 1:5, NKJV). Contrary to what certain feminist theologians think, God is the Lord of creation, not its midwife. God did not need to create something outside himself as an object for his love, for *God is love* (1 John 4:8). There is nothing missing or lacking in God. He is the fountain of being. In him dwell all holiness, glory, light, power, happiness, and joy. Yet amazingly, out of the richness and utter sufficiency of his own being, God created the world and human beings within it. He granted them a creaturely reality and freedom and invited them to share in the out-splashing of his divine love for all eternity. Indeed, the Bible speaks of God as "jealous" for his own glory and honor. He will brook no rivals. But he is not a grudging, stingy God like a Silas Marner (in George Eliot's novel) carefully counting his gold coins every night for fear that one of them might have gotten away. No, at the heart of God springs freedom, an unthreatenedness, a generosity that reflects his own character. This forms the basis of all human reality and freedom. This kindles the source of wonder and awe, the kind of wonder that prompted Martin Luther to find sermons in peach stones and to adore the living God who made heaven and earth (and me too, Luther says) of his "sheer fatherly kindness and compassion, apart from any merit or worthiness of mine: For all of which I am bound to thank and praise him, to serve him and to be obedient, which is assuredly true."[6]

Some people accept the idea that God created the world, but they cannot imagine that he has much to do with its continuing operation, much less with our human lives. The British poet and novelist, Thomas Hardy, once wrote in disparaging terms about God as

> . . . the dreaming, dark, dumb Thing
> That turns the handle of this idle Show.[7]

Hardy believed in the god of deism: he created the world and still cranks it along from time to time, but he wouldn't think of getting his hands dirty in the daily muck and mess of it all. He is like an absentee landlord who neither knows nor cares much about the tenants who occupy his property. An idol of the modern imagination, this god has crippled feet and withered hands, eyes that don't see, and ears that don't hear.

How different is the God of the Bible who is everywhere active, alive, involved. Jesus said that no act is too insignificant for the Father's care. He knows every time a sparrow falls to the ground in a hailstorm. In his great and boundless wisdom, God knows even how to use evil instruments to do good, including the Devil himself. Paul makes this clear in 2 Corinthians 12:7, where he describes his "thorn . . . in the flesh" as something "given" by God through the agency of

Satan. Through God's providential care, even painful episodes such as this can become occasions for grace.

COMMON GRACE

When we think of God's general providence and care for the world and all its creatures, we are talking about *common grace* as distinguished from the *special grace* of God manifested in the coming of Christ into the world to save sinners. We can see evidence of God's common grace in his general revelation—God's disclosure of his reality throughout the created world and also in the human conscience. In speaking to a pagan audience at Lystra, Paul declared that God "did not leave himself without witness, for he did good by giving you rains from heaven and fruitful seasons, satisfying your hearts with food and gladness" (Acts 14:17). God pours his common grace out indiscriminately on all persons everywhere, causing the sun to shine and the rain to fall on the just and the unjust alike (see Matt. 5:45).

God's common grace also serves as a restraining force against the demonic powers of evil that, if left to their own devices, would wreak such havoc on earth that human life would be utterly impossible. All political order, social stability, and family cohesiveness would be overturned in a moment without the nurture of God's sustaining grace. In this sense, Paul refers to government as an authority "appointed" by God. A civil ruler is "God's servant," that is, his agent for equity and justice in the world (Rom. 13:2–4), even though civil authorities may have no personal knowledge of God as Redeemer. All that is good and tolerable in human life, all that is noble and praiseworthy in the realms of politics, culture, science, art, music, literature—for all of this we may thank God for his common grace, reflected in his "longsuffering" and patience toward his wayward creation (see 2 Pet. 3:9, NKJV).

Some teach that common grace and general revelation alone are sufficient to bring lost persons into a saving relationship with God. However, nothing in the Bible supports this theory. On the contrary, the Scriptures teach that human beings everywhere have abused and corrupted the natural knowledge of God implanted in their souls. Again and again, they have turned from the knowledge of God revealed in nature and in conscience and have worshiped and served false gods, idols, even demons rather than submitting to the one true and living God of creation (see Rom. 1:18–31). This was as true in the Old Testament as it is in the New, as the prophet Isaiah made clear:

> Though grace is shown to the wicked,
>> they do not learn righteousness;
> even in a land of uprightness they go on doing evil
>> and regard not the majesty of the LORD. (Isa. 26:10, NIV)

The verdict of Scripture is clear: God's presence and power are evidenced in every human heart through the witness of common grace. This testimony renders every single person inexcusable before the bar of God's righteous judgment. But true salvation and eternal life—that is, deliverance from sin and death—come about only through the interposition of God's special, redemptive grace.

GOD'S LONG-RANGE PLAN

Oscar Hardman once wrote that the doctrine of grace "is profound in its nature, wide in its scope, comprehensive in its bearings, forbidding in its possession of a technical terminology, and confusing in the variety of the formulations which its successive exponents have given to it."[8] Surely he is right! Even Paul, the great apostle of grace, often stretches the capacity of human language to its breaking point in describing the boundless love and grace of God. Right in the middle of his letter to the Ephesians, he interrupts his discussion of salvation by grace to conduct a prayer meeting. He actually falls on his knees and prays to the Father. He asks that the Christians to whom he is writing may be able to grasp the extravagant dimensions of his subject. Who can experience its breadth, he asks? Or measure its length, or plumb its depths, or soar up to its heights? He wants them to understand the full extent of God's grace, not just intellectually, but experientially. He wants them "to know it, though it is beyond knowledge" (Eph. 3:19, NEB).

One of the grandest statements of the overarching structure of divine grace comes at the very beginning of Ephesians. Here Paul describes its comprehensive content and its encompassing reach. Ephesians 1:3–14 is just one sentence in the Greek New Testament, perhaps the longest sentence in the Bible! So rich and complex is Paul's thought here that one struggles to translate this as a single sentence in English. The King James Version, using lots of colons, divides it into three complete sentences; the New International Version, seven. This is how Eugene H. Peterson renders this sentence in his popular paraphrase, *The Message*:

> How blessed is God! And what a blessing he is! He's the Father of our Master, Jesus Christ, and takes us to the high places of blessing in him. Long before he laid down earth's foundations, he had us in mind, had settled on us as the focus of his love, to be made whole and holy by his love. Long, long ago he decided to adopt us into his family through Jesus Christ. (What pleasure he took in planning this!) He wanted us to enter into the celebration of his lavish gift-giving by the hand of his beloved Son.
>
> Because of the sacrifice of the Messiah, his blood poured out on the altar of the Cross, we're a free people—free of penalties and punishments chalked up by all our misdeeds. And not just barely free, either. *Abundantly* free! He thought of everything, provided for everything we could possibly need, letting us in on the plans he took such delight in making. He set it all out before us in Christ, a long-range plan in which everything would be brought together and summed up in him, everything in deepest heaven, everything on planet earth.

It's in Christ that we find out who we are and what we are living for. Long before we first heard of Christ and got our hopes up, he had his eye on us, had designs on us for glorious living, part of the overall purpose he is working out in everything and everyone.

It's in Christ that you, once you heard the truth and believed it (this Message of your salvation), found yourselves home free—signed, sealed, and delivered by the Holy Spirit. This signet from God is the first installment on what's coming, a reminder that we'll get everything God has planned for us, a praising and glorious life. (Eph. 1:3–14)

This passage begins and ends with praise to God. In between Paul places our Christian calling and everything related to it in the context of God's eternal purpose—his long-range plan stretching from the very first nanosecond of creation through the final cry of victory at the end of time. He does this by identifying four "moments" in God's plan of salvation. We can depict Paul's theology of grace as a continuum with four distinct but interrelated moments that derive both their unity and their uniqueness from God's free and sovereign grace. If, for the sake of clarity, we call these moments *metahistorical*, *historical*, *experiential*, and *eschatological*, then the continuum may be illustrated as in figure 1.

Fig. 1

Metahistorical	Historical	Experiential	Eschatological
⬇	⬇	⬇	⬇
Election	Redemption	Vocation	Perseverance
⬇	⬇	⬇	
God's Decrees	Atonement	Regeneration	
		⬇	
		Repentance, Faith	
		⬇	
		Assurance	

Let's look briefly at each of these four ways of situating grace within the overall plan of salvation.

Metahistorical

The word *metahistorical* means "above history" or "prior to history." Paul says that God established his purpose of grace even before the creation of the world: "Long before he laid down earth's foundations, he had us in mind, had settled on us as the focus of his love, to be made whole and holy by his love" (Eph. 1:4–5, MESSAGE). Admittedly, eternity remains a difficult topic for a finite mind to grasp, and we must be careful not to speculate beyond what God has revealed to us in his Word. An eager student once asked Augustine what he thought God was doing before he made the world. The great theologian replied, with a twinkle in his eye perhaps, that God was busy creating hell for overly curious souls! Certainly there is much about the eternal decrees (the technical term for God's pretemporal decisions) about which we do not know and may never learn this side of heaven.

But from time to time throughout the Bible, God himself pulls back the curtain of eternity and gives us a glimpse into the inner sanctum of his divine life in eternity past. For example, Jesus spoke of the intimate relationship he enjoyed with the Father "before the world existed" (John 17:5, 24). Jesus also declared that God had been preparing a kingdom for his elect children "from the foundation of the world" (Matt. 25:34). Peter tells us that Christ was foreordained "before the foundation of the world" to be a spotless sacrifice for sin (1 Pet. 1:18–20). John repeats this idea in Revelation 13:8, where he portrays Jesus as "the Lamb that was slain from the creation of the world" (NIV). Together these verses tell us that God saves men and women not on the basis of their merits, good works, or anything else they have done. He saves humankind in accordance with his predetermined plan, his gracious election, the central focus of which is

Jesus Christ. Believers are predestined only "in Christ," never apart from Christ.

Historical

What God decided and planned to do before the creation of the world, he has in fact accomplished in time and space. The drama of redemption unfolds throughout the Bible from the first messianic prophecy in Genesis 3:15, all the way through the Old Testament to the anguished cry of Golgotha, "My God, my God, why have you forsaken me?" (Matt. 27:46). On the cross Jesus bore the unmitigated penalty and damnation of sin and, standing in our place, satisfied the righteous demands of God's justice. "The LORD has laid on him the iniquity of us all," Isaiah said in prophetic foresight (Isa. 53:6). The meaning of the cross, and its power too, were released by Jesus' resurrection from the dead, followed by his ascension back to heaven, and his pouring forth of the Holy Spirit on the Day of Pentecost. All of this is the result of God's grace, "his lavish gift-giving by the hand of his beloved Son" (Eph. 1:6, MESSAGE).

Some people teach that God had devised a way of salvation for the Old Testament saints based on law and then came up with a different one for New Testament believers founded on grace. But this presents a serious misunderstanding of God's redemptive work. It is certainly true that Jesus is an incomparably greater King than Solomon, and that he promulgated an infinitely better covenant than Moses. But throughout history, God has had one and only one plan of salvation for everybody everywhere—by grace alone, through faith alone, in Jesus Christ alone! True enough, the Old Testament saints saw only dimly and from afar what we now can look back upon and see clearly through the lenses of Calvary and Easter Sunday. But salvation was by grace for them no less than it is for us. In proclaiming this law-free gospel before the Council at Jerusalem, the apostle Peter declared that salvation was, as it always had been, by grace alone: "Now then, why do you try to test God by putting on the necks of the disciples a yoke that neither we nor our fathers have been able to bear? No! We believe it is through the grace of our Lord Jesus that we are saved, *just as they are*" (Acts 15:10–11, NIV).

Experiential

By "experiential" I mean the personal, existential appropriation of Christ's redeeming work in the life of the believer. John Calvin put it this way: "As long as Christ remains outside of us, and we are separated from him, all that he has suffered and done for the salvation of the human race remains useless and of no value to us."[9] The experiential aspect of the economy of grace includes what the New Testament calls our vocation or calling. This has both an outward and an inner dimension. These two are brought together in Ephesians 1:13–14. We are called externally through the faithful proclamation of the good news: "And you also were included in Christ when you heard the word of truth, the gospel of your salvation" (NIV). Inwardly, we are called by the Holy Spirit, who regenerates us (the new birth) as we repent of our sins and trust in Christ.

Having been justified and forgiven, Christians can live confidently in the assurance that they are in a right standing with God and that this will result in their spending eternity with him in heaven: "Having believed, you were marked in [Christ] with a seal, the promised Holy Spirit, who is a deposit guaranteeing our inheritance" (NIV). Nikolaus Ludwig von Zinzendorf, the founder of the Moravians, captured this note of Christian assurance in his charming hymn:

> Bold shall I stand in that great day,
> For who aught to my charge shall lay?
> While by my Lord absolved I am,
> From sin's tremendous curse and blame.[10]

Eschatological

In his majestic overview of the operations of grace from eternity to eternity in Ephesians 1:3–14, Paul does not stop at the point of death, when the believer is united with Christ in heaven, nor even with the second coming of Christ—the rapture, the resurrection, the millennial reign of Jesus on earth. No, he looks beyond all of these great events to the final consummation of all things, to the moment when God's intended purpose in eternity past shall have been completely fulfilled. In the final consummation, all things in heaven and on earth will be brought together under one Head, even Christ (Eph. 1:10).

The Greek word for "bringing all things together" is *apokatastasis*, the longest word in the Greek New Testament. It refers to the ultimate wrapping up of human history, to God's cosmic victory over all the forces of evil. When this occurs, everyone in the universe, not only Christians but also unbelievers who have died rejecting the love of Christ, together with the angels in heaven and the demons in hell, will exclaim together (what the Bible says is already true) that Jesus Christ is Lord of lords and King of kings! And all of this is by grace too! What a great comfort to know that God's purpose will not be thwarted. In the meantime, all truly regenerated believers have been granted the gift of perseverance. We can celebrate our present and future security in the knowledge that, at the end of the day, every foe in heaven and on earth will be vanquished by the almighty love of God. God will certainly complete the "good work" that he has begun in the lives of those he has redeemed (Phil. 1:6; 2:5–11).

GRACE IN DEPTH

In this sweeping overview we have seen something of the "length and breadth" of God's dazzling, amazing grace as outlined in the Bible's story line from its origin in the eternal decrees through its final fulfill- ment at the end of time. This important perspective reminds us that grace is not an impersonal force or even a divine quality to be analyzed and studied abstractly. No, grace means God himself is operating in love to the praise of his glory. As Martin Luther once said, grace is God's middle name!

But, at the heart of the gospel itself lies a "depth" dimension to grace. God's sufficient grace radiates its adequacy to meet the deepest needs of the vilest sinner who ever lived. There is no hell on earth so deep but that God's grace can go deeper still. Thus, the New Testament states that Jesus "is able to save to the uttermost those who draw near to God through him" (Heb. 7:25). We experience grace on many different levels in our lives, including these:

- We experience grace as *pardon*. God's forgiveness and justification remove our guilty standing before him—our real guilt, not just our guilty feelings. The psalmist claims that God's pardoning grace removes our guilt of sin "as far as the east is from the west" (Ps. 103:12).
- We experience grace as *acceptance*. In Christ we who were distant from God, covered with shame, have been embraced, welcomed, and accepted—not because we are acceptable, but solely because we are loved.
- We experience grace as *joy*. This delivers us from the frantic quest to be "happy" through stuffing our lives with fleeting pleasures and "joyrides" that only leave us sadder, more depressed. Real joy comes from knowing God and serving him.
- We experience grace as *peace*. God's *shalom* answers the anxieties and insecurities that threaten us from every side. The standard New Testament greeting is "grace and peace." Grace and peace are twins; they belong together, related as cause and effect.

- We experience grace as *power*. Most people do not so much lack the knowledge to live as they should as they do the ability to carry out what they already know is right. God's grace acts as an antidote to our impotence. It transforms, energizes, enables.
- We experience grace as *hope*. This is hope not in the loose sense of a vague general wish that may not come true, as in "hopefully it won't rain tomorrow." In Titus 2:11–13, Paul connects the grace of God with the "blessed hope" of Jesus' return in glory, a great motivation for confident Christian living.
- We experience grace as *love*. God's grace and love are so close that, at times, we cannot distinguish them. The Bible says that "perfect love casts out fear" (1 John 4:18), and God's gracious love counters the nagging fears and doubts all of us have.
- We experience grace as *gratitude*. The most basic response we can make to grace remains a life of thank-yous to God. As Lewis Smedes points out, true gratitude involves "a sense of wonder and sometimes elation at the lavish generosity of God."[11]

Later in this study, we will look at the way grace has been understood throughout the history of the church, including some of the controversies it has generated among believers through the ages. But we must never forget that, first and foremost, grace is not something to be studied, analyzed, and argued about; it is rather something to be received, experienced, and changed by.

Two

THE PROVIDENCE MYSTERY

It is the great support and solace of the saints in all the distresses that befall them here, that there is a wise Spirit sitting in all the wheels of motion, and governing the most eccentric creatures and their most pernicious designs to blessed and happy issues. And, indeed, it were not worthwhile to live in a world devoid of God and providence.[1] ~ JOHN FLAVEL

There are many things Christians believe simply because they are undeniably taught in the Bible. Yet we cannot remove all questions and puzzlements. We cannot explain with precision how these things can be true in terms of human reason and logic. Consider the doctrine of the Holy Trinity. Orthodox Christians of all confessions believe in the Trinity. We believe that the one true God is, and from all eternity has ever been, the Father, the Son, and the Holy Spirit. Yet, we ask, how can God be one and three at the same time? Or consider the fact of the incarnation. Nothing is more central to the gospel itself than John 1:14: "The Word became flesh and dwelt among us." It's a stupendous thought—the Creator of heaven and earth tethered to a human umbilical cord! How can this be, we wonder? How do we explain that Jesus was fully divine, "very God of very God," as the Nicene Creed declares, and yet at the same time completely human with genes, chromosomes, and DNA molecules of his own, with eyes that cried real tears and toes that turned blue when he stubbed them?

Or, how about this: We believe that God is absolutely sovereign over all that he has made. And we also believe that he has given free moral agency and responsibility to the men and women created in his image. How can this be? Keep this question in mind as we examine what the Bible teaches about the providence of God—the way God sustains and governs the world and moves it along, guiding it moment by moment, toward its appointed end.

Before we consider the question of providence, let's look at four words that are often used when we ponder the difficult questions that baffle the human mind, issues such as the Trinity or christology or the relationship between predestination and human freedom. The four words are

- *Contradiction.* A contradiction is a condition in which at least two things are at variance, that is, truly contrary to one another. A real contradiction involves a genuine discrepancy, not merely an apparent inconsistency or disagreement. In the garden of Eden, God told Adam and Eve that death would be the penalty for eating the forbidden fruit. When Satan said, "You will not surely die," he contradicted God (Gen. 3:4).
- *Antinomy.* An antinomy is a combination of two thoughts or principles, each perfectly true in its own right, that we cannot harmonize in our minds. J. I. Packer uses the example of light as an antinomy in modern physics. Does light consist of waves or particles? Good evidence sup-

ports both views, and both must be treated as true even though they seem incompatible with our current understanding of the universe.

- *Paradox.* Having a meaning close to that of *antinomy*, the word *paradox* is sometimes used as synonymous with it, but there is an important distinction. Some scholars believe a paradox (from the Greek *para*, "beyond," and *doxa*, "opinion" or "belief") appears to be a contradiction. It seems to be something absurd, but when we look closer, it proves to be true in fact. For example, when Paul says "When I am weak, then I am strong" (2 Cor. 12:10), he is speaking paradoxically, for his words are quite comprehensible, though still jarring, once we understand his intended use of them.

- *Mystery.* The term *mystery* refers to a whole complex of ideas, including antinomies and paradoxes perhaps, that we know on good grounds to be true, but that are inexplicable or inscrutable. *Mystery* literally means something that has been kept secret. In theology, a mystery is an assumed truth that the human mind cannot comprehend but must accept by faith.

Christians are those who have already glimpsed something of the unfathomable "mystery" of God's will in Christ (Eph. 1:9; see also Rom. 16:25–27), as we have seen in Paul's depiction of God's great purpose of grace. By his mercy and grace, God has let us in on his secret plan. And yet there is much that we do not know. We have not yet arrived. We don't yet see "face to face," but only partially, dimly. Sometimes life seems like a jigsaw puzzle with some of the pieces missing. "At present we are looking at puzzling reflections in a mirror.... At present all I know is a little fraction of the truth" (1 Cor. 13:12, PHILLIPS). For this reason Christians walk through life by faith, not by sight. Only

God is omniscient. We know some things surely, but we don't know everything for sure. We have been saved, and yet we still suffer. We live in hope for we are not exempt from the "groanings" of the fallen world around us. "For in this hope we were saved. Now hope that is seen is not hope. For who hopes for what he sees? But if we hope for what we do not see, we wait for it with patience" (Rom. 8:24–25).

THE DOCTRINE OF PROVIDENCE

What is divine providence? Let's look at two classic definitions of providence from the Baptist heritage. The first comes from a seventeenth-century confession of faith called The Orthodox Creed, published by General or Arminian Baptists in 1679:

> The Almighty God that created all things and gave them their being
> by his infinite power and wisdom, doth sustain and uphold and move,
> direct, dispose, and govern all creatures and things from the greatest
> to the least, according to the counsel of his own good will and pleasure,
> for his own glory and his creatures' good.[2]

The second definition comes from the first confessional statement published by Southern Baptists after the founding of the Southern Baptist Convention in 1845. We call this the Abstract of Principles. It is still used as the primary doctrinal standard (and subscribed by all professors) in two of that denomination's seminaries:

> God from eternity decrees or permits all things that come to pass, and
> perpetually upholds, directs and governs all creatures and all events; yet
> so as not in any wise to be the author or approver of sin nor to destroy
> the free will and responsibility of intelligent creatures.[3]

These quotations show that, despite their different understandings about some matters (such as predestination and the possibility of losing one's salvation), Baptists with both Arminian and Calvinistic leanings are largely agreed in their teaching about divine providence. Here is common ground on which we can stand united.

We can summarize the general thrust of these two statements in three affirmations:

Nothing Exists except in Some Relationship to God

At the heart of biblical faith stands the doctrine of creation "out of nothing" (*ex nihilo* in Latin). God didn't make the world out of some kind of primordial matter, matter that already existed. Plato depicted him doing this in the *Timaeus*—an Artisan shaping the world out of a kind of cosmic modeling clay. This is not the biblical view of creation. No, God spoke, and things that did not previously exist came into being. Every molecule or atom in the universe owes its origin to the sovereign Lord of time and eternity. The twenty-four elders in heaven acknowledge this truth when they sing,

> Worthy are you, our Lord and God,
> > to receive glory and honor and power,
> for you created *all things*,
> > and by your will they existed and were created. (Rev. 4:11)

God created all things, visible and invisible. Heaven, too, is a created place, along with the angels and other heavenly beings. The prayer of Ezra in Nehemiah 9:6 clearly connects creation and providence: "You are the LORD, you alone. You have made heaven, the heaven of heavens, with all their host, the earth and all that is on it, the seas and all that is in them; and you preserve all of them; and the host of heaven worships you." As Dale Moody put it, "Belief in God as creator denies self-existence to things. Things are dependent upon God not only in their origin but also in their continuation and consummation. The action of God in the continuation of creation is his work of preservation."[4]

Nothing Happens apart from God's Purposeful Activity

When the Abstract of Principles declares that God "decrees or permits all things that come to pass," it simply echoes the clear teaching of the Bible. The Psalms are filled with affirmations of God's comprehensive providence:

> The LORD has established his throne in the heavens,
>> and his kingdom rules over all. (Ps. 103:19)

And again:

> For I know that the LORD is great,
>> and that our Lord is above all gods.
> Whatever the LORD pleases, he does,
>> in heaven and on earth,
>> in the seas and all deeps.
> He it is who makes the clouds rise at the end of the earth,
>> who makes lightnings for the rain
>> and brings forth the wind from his storehouses. (Ps. 135:5–7)

To us, it might seem that things happen by chance, at random. "Oh, that was an accident," we say. But there are no accidents with God. Even events like rolling dice or flipping coins are ordered by him, as Proverbs 16:33 makes clear:

> The lot is cast into the lap,
>> but its every decision is from the LORD.

This is why Paul can state so boldly that God "works *all things* according to the counsel of his will" (Eph. 1:11).

Nothing Can Thwart God's Gracious Design in Christ

We cannot think of providence apart from Jesus Christ. Through him, God made everything in heaven and on earth (John 1:3). He continually "upholds the universe by the word of his power" (Heb. 1:3). Jesus remains the eternal divine agent in both creation and providence: "In him," Paul says, "all things hold together" (Col. 1:17). God has "put all things in subjection under his feet" and, amid all the ambiguities of history, he is guiding the world and everything within it toward its divinely appointed end, so that ultimately "Jesus is Lord" will be on the lips of every sentient being from heaven down to hell (see Phil. 2:5–10).

INTERVENING AND INTERWEAVING

This is a sweeping view of God as the sovereign disposer of all that is—a theology of God without any loose ends. No honest reading of the Bible allows anything else, and we have sampled only a fraction of the thousands of passages that underscore this truth. But, we ask, does such a view leave enough "elbow room" for meaningful human participation within the orders of creation? Don't God's sovereignty and providence devour human responsibility and undercut all morality?

At this point let us recall everything said in chapter 1 about the gracious character of God. God is omnipotent—all-powerful. He is also omnibenevolent, all-loving. *God is love*—love is his very essence. We will return to this theme when we look at the difference between the biblical view of God's providential governance and various forms of fatalism or determinism. The God of the Bible is not a God of brute force or arrogant self-will. That is a better definition of the Devil, for it was Satan who kept on saying, "I will . . . I will . . . I will" (Isa. 14:12–15). No, the God of the covenant, the God whom Jesus taught us to call "Abba," is kind and generous. In his utter holiness, he is a

God of never-failing mercy and compassion. We are amazed at his forbearance, at his extravagant grace and inexpressible love. Can we do anything less than say with the children of Israel, "Give thanks to the LORD, for he is good, for his steadfast love endures forever" (Ps. 136:1)? We must keep this in mind when we acknowledge that "God's works of providence are his most holy, wise, and powerful preserving and governing all his creatures, and all their actions" (see Westminster Shorter Catechism, Q. 11).

The Bible undoubtedly teaches divine sovereignty—but that is only one side of the antinomy. It also makes room for human freedom and accountability. Psalm 47:2, "For the LORD, the Most High, is to be feared, a great king over all the earth," is answered by Psalm 138:6, "Though the LORD is high, he regards the lowly." Just as many texts in the Bible teach human responsibility as teach divine sovereignty. Again and again through the prophets, God pleads for his people to repent, to turn from their wicked ways, and to seek his face. Many times the children of Israel are confronted with words such as these: "The LORD is with you while you are with him. If you seek him, he will be found by you, but if you forsake him, he will forsake you" (2 Chron. 15:2). God may harden Pharaoh's heart, but even that wicked ruler was not an unthinking puppet. Far from it—he was a malicious evildoer whom God held accountable. In the New Testament, Jesus wept over the city of Jerusalem and exclaimed, "How often I have longed to gather your children together, as a hen gathers her chicks under her wings, *but you were not willing!*" (Luke 13:34, NIV). The sin and rejection of Jerusalem's people could not thwart Christ's salvific mission, but their free moral agency was not extinguished by Jesus' march to Calvary. Their choice to spurn the Savior's love was tragically all too real.

Granted, the Bible affirms both God's sovereignty and human free agency in the course of events. But how is it that God accomplishes his providential purposes within the world? The answer is twofold: Sometimes by *intervening* directly, immediately, miraculously. More often, though, by *interweaving* his guidance and rule with the intentions and freely chosen acts of human beings. Numerous examples of God's radical intervention in the lives of his people and in the course of nature fill the Bible. He sent the flood as an expression of his judgment. He visited Egypt with plagues and rescued Israel from the clutches of Pharaoh "with a mighty hand" (Deut. 7:8). He smote the army of the Assyrians, leaving many thousands dead. He healed the sick and raised the dead. He engineered Peter's miraculous escape from prison and rescued Jonah from a seafaring death. When God acts in such a swift and unilateral way, we stand amazed, as when Moses and the children of Israel sang of the intervening hand of God in the exodus:

> Who is like you, O LORD, among the gods?
> Who is like you, majestic in holiness,
> awesome in glorious deeds, doing wonders? (Ex. 15:11)

Even more frequently, though, we see the hand of God in the interlacing of divine and human activity. After the children of Israel languished for years in exile, God allowed them to return to their homeland through the intervention of Cyrus, the ruler of Persia. Their release was Cyrus's idea; under no compulsion or constraint, he freely chose to liberate the Israelites and send them home. Yet when the prophet Isaiah considered this momentous event, he ascribed it to God:

> Who has performed and done this . . . ?
> I, . . . I am he. (Isa. 41:4)

Clearly God worked through Cyrus. We can even say that God used Cyrus, including his freely chosen decisions, to accomplish what he had intended (and promised) to do beforehand.

The death of Christ is another example of how God's providence works in and through freely chosen human acts. Jesus was the Lamb of God who was slain from the foundation of the world. The shadow of the cross fell over every event of his life from Bethlehem to Calvary. For centuries the prophets had predicted the sacrificial atoning death of the Messiah, as Jesus himself acknowledged: "Was it not necessary that the Christ should suffer these things . . . ?" (Luke 24:26). Clearly Jesus was put to death at the hands of cruel men who tortured and crucified him outside the gates of Jerusalem. The crucifiers were not marionettes dancing on a string. They were free moral agents fully accountable for their heinous deeds. Peter made this clear in his sermon on the day of Pentecost: "This Jesus, delivered up according to the definite plan and foreknowledge of God, you crucified and killed by the hands of lawless men" (Acts 2:23). Here, in the same verse, Peter attributes the one event of Jesus' death to two centers of intentionality: God's definite plan, and the hands of lawless men. This motif was so pervasive among the earliest Christians that they incorporated it into their prayer life (Acts 4:27–28): "Indeed Herod and Pontius Pilate met together with the Gentiles and the people of Israel in this city to conspire against your holy servant Jesus, whom you anointed. *They did what your power and will had decided beforehand should happen*" (NIV).

You (God) had *decided* . . . and they *did*!

Note carefully that the Bible never explains *how* the sinful acts of wicked men coalesce with God's sovereign purpose, but somehow mysteriously they do work together concurrently. G. K. Chesterton observed that "Christianity got over the difficulty of combining furious opposites, by keeping them both, and keeping them both furious."[5] Our finite human minds cannot comprehend such an antinomy. We are tempted to resolve it either by qualifying God's sovereignty or by denying human free agency. While this solution is neater logically, it could never be acceptable biblically. To be faithful to what God has revealed about how he works in the affairs of this world, we must say both–and, not either–or.

FOUR DEAD ENDS

We must distinguish the biblical view of providence from several competing perspectives that, however popular in some circles, do not square with the evidence of Scripture.

1. Deism. Deists believe that God, having constructed the world in the beginning, has since then left it to run its course more or less on its own. The God of deism is high and mighty, transcendent and aloof, distant and removed from the goings-on of everyday life. Deism denies to God what the Bible everywhere attributes—a watchful, effective, active, ceaseless engagement with the governance of the world he has created. Deism depersonalizes God. It gives us omnipotence without the Almighty, sovereignty apart from the Sovereign. No wonder deism has become, for many, a way station on the road to atheism! If God is seen merely as the First Cause, or the Final Force, the Cosmic Glue that holds it all together, then he can be quite easily dispensed with in the interest of secular naturalism. Today, deism as a system of thought is a spent force, but, as Wayne Grudem has noted, "Many . . . nominal Christians today are, in effect, practical deists, since they live lives almost totally devoid of genuine prayer, worship, fear of God, or moment-by-moment trust in God to care for needs that arise."[6]

2. Pantheism. Pantheism stands at the opposite extreme from deism. It equates God and the created order by claiming that God is everything and everything is God. Deism makes God transcendent and removes him far away from the affairs of daily life. Pantheism makes God utterly immanent, collapsing all distinction between the Creator and the creature. God is no longer personal in any sense but merely the manifestation of all laws, forces, and principles of the self-existing universe. Today's New Age spirituality shows a strong pantheistic current when its "believers" worship nature, the earth, the cosmos, or "the god/goddess within."

3. *Fatalism.* The biblical doctrine of providence is vastly different from a heartless determinism or fatalism. Fatalism teaches that everything is entirely determined by an inviolable sequence of cause and effect. Thus every event we "choose" to do—from casting a vote to brushing our teeth—is not free but determined by a sequence of causes independent of our will. Some forms of fatalism teach that human destiny is linked with the stars. This is why so many people read the daily horoscope with religious fervor, hoping to discover the secret to romance or riches. Among the world religions, Islam is known for its necessitarian theology, while atheistic determinism undergirds many modern approaches to human life, such as behaviorist psychology and Freudian psychoanalysis. But the Bible never presents God's providence as a scheme of strict determinism. God "makes room" for the creatures he has made in his own image. He has endowed them with creaturely freedom, even though he knows in advance that they will misuse it to their own detriment. As the Abstract of Principles puts it, God never destroys "the free will and responsibility of intelligent creatures." On the contrary, God works *in* and *through* all freely chosen human decisions, including quite horrible ones, such as the decision of Pilate and the Jewish religious leaders to crucify Jesus, which God used as a means to accomplish the redemptive purpose he planned from all eternity.

G. K. Berkouwer explains the difference between the Christian view of providence and deterministic fatalism in this way:

> Divine determining is utterly different from what is generally understood
> by determinism. It is not that there is a material similarity between

the confession of God's providence and determinism and that the only difference between them is the formal difference that in determinism the first cause stands at the end of the series of causes, while in the confession of providence *God* stands there. Since we have to do with the providence of *God*, everything else, including planning, determining, and acting, is different. This is why we never find in the Scriptures either the rigidity or the violence typical of determinism. In the confession of God's almighty power, the personal, living God is confessed. Responsibility is not crowded out by his power; neither is the meaning of guilt and punishment. We are deeply conscious of the impossibility of our discerning the relation between the divine activity and ours, but we are able to see in Scripture that the incomparable enterprise of God is in its divine character so great and majestic that it can embrace human freedom and responsibility within itself without being thereby assaulted or even limited.[7]

4. Process theism. In its starkest form, process theism denies the sovereignty of God by positing another reality alongside God by which he is necessarily limited—matter perhaps, or the universe, or chaos. A somewhat softer form of process thinking has gained currency in recent years under the banner of "the openness of God." This view denies that God has exhaustive knowledge of the future because, so the theory runs, the future is not really "there" to be known, even by God! While pretending to "protect" God against a false view of sovereignty that would exclude him from all meaningful interaction within the realm of space and time, this so-called open view of God actually reduces God to the creaturely level by closing off both the reality of predictive prophecy and the urgency of petitionary prayer. Process theology, in all its forms, remains a dangerous deviation from historic Christian orthodoxy. It has been repudiated through the centuries by Calvinists, Arminians, Protestants, and Catholics alike.

LESSONS FROM PROVIDENCE

Meditation on the ways of God serves as an important spiritual discipline in the lives of Christians. It is a mark of Christian maturity to confess with the psalmist that "the LORD is righteous in all his ways, and holy in all his works" (Ps. 145:17, KJV). We must be aware of false perspectives and theological dead ends lest we be robbed of the great comfort God has for us in the doctrine of providence. Our consideration of this theme, however, is not a matter of philosophical speculation or theological argument. Our faith should be strengthened as we consider how our lives are governed by the wisdom and care of our loving heavenly Father. As J. B. Phillips renders Romans 8:28, "We know that to those who love God, who are called according to his plan, everything that happens fits into a pattern for good." We can learn many things from the study of providence, including these five principles:

1. The doctrine of providence reminds us that God is the sovereign Lord of history. The God of the Bible is a "hands-on" God, intimately concerned with the smallest details of our lives. But he is also the Creator and Judge of the world, which he is infallibly guiding toward its predestined goal. Theologians sometimes distinguish God's *special providence*, which relates to the salvation and care of his chosen people, from God's *general providence* (comparable to common grace), through which he governs the courses of nature and history. This is a helpful distinction in some ways, but we should not press it too far. As we saw in the example of Cyrus, secular and sacred are mysteriously intermingled in the unfolding drama of redemption. God used the events of so-called secular history to prepare the way for the coming of Christ, who was born "when the fullness of time had come" (Gal. 4:4). And he still sustains and guides the church through all the ups and downs of historical change and conflict.

Textbooks on history often read as though politics and economics are the decisive determiners in the course of history: wars are won by those who have the best diplomats or the biggest bombs; prosperity hinges on this or that economic system. The Bible, however, tells us that another hidden, often invisible, factor needs to be considered: The hand of God. As Daniel 5:21 puts it, "The Most High God rules the kingdom of mankind and sets over it whom he will." Again, Proverbs 21:1,

> The king's heart is a stream of water in the hand of the LORD;
>> he turns it wherever he will.

God sometimes uses even evil and tyrannical powers to accomplish his purposes. The rise and fall of nations and empires does not happen apart from God's superintendence. It is he "who executes judgment, putting down one and lifting up another" (Ps. 75:7).

Because God is the Lord of history, Christians must not give unqualified allegiance to any earthly power or political regime. Of course, we should love our country and pray for our leaders, but let us be wary of equating political success with divine favor. In the 1930s many German Christians forgot this principle. Swept along in the rising tide of Nazism, a group of German Protestant theologians made this statement in 1934: "We are full of thanks to God that he, as Lord of history, has given us Adolf Hitler, our leader and savior from our difficult lot. We acknowledge that we, with body and soul, are bound and dedicated to the German state and to its *Führer*."[8]

How different was the witness of Martin Niemöller, a Lutheran pastor imprisoned by the Gestapo for his opposition to the Nazi state. On one occasion, when he was being ridiculed and taunted by Hitler himself, he reminded the dictator, echoing the words of Jesus before Pilate, you have no authority except what God has given to you, and one day things will look different when both of us stand before the bar of God's judgment. Today, when many Christians are still persecuted for their faith, it is a great comfort to know that God's cause is not in doubt. His purpose of grace will triumph over Satan and all his pomp.

2. *We often see the pattern of providence only in retrospect.* William Cowper's great hymn on providence, "God Moves in a Mysterious Way," contains these lines:

> Judge not the Lord by feeble sense,
> But trust Him for His grace;
> Behind a frowning providence
> He hides a smiling face.

> Blind unbelief is sure to err,
> And scan His work in vain,
> God is His own interpreter,
> And He will make it plain.[9]

The "making plain" part baffles many Christians. When we are overcome by grief or confronted with a tragic event either in our own life or in that of a loved one, we seldom see how these experiences fit into God's plan for us. But when we look back over our lives from the perspective of, say, five years, or ten, or twenty or more, we can understand more clearly some of those things that at the time brought only tears and questions.

Remember the biblical story of Joseph? On one level it is a simple plot. Mean brothers betray a spoiled-brat kid. They send him to a foreign country as a slave. There, after being falsely accused of a crime he did not commit, he goes to prison with no hope of release. Surely, from the pit and then the prison, Joseph must have wondered about the goodness of a God who could have allowed such things to happen to him. *Why me? Why has this happened to me?* He could see no purposive meaning in these events. But later on, when he discloses his true identity to his brothers, he makes an astonishing statement: "It was not you who sent me here, but God. . . . You intended to harm me but God intended it for good to accomplish what is now being done, the saving of many lives" (Gen. 45:8; 50:20, NIV).

Note carefully: not only did God permit what occurred, but he actually *intended* it. He "meant" it, as the KJV and several other versions have it. What Joseph's brothers did, of course, was wicked in every respect. They were not absolved of responsibility for their treachery. But God in his sovereignty was also at work even in that horrible circumstance to accomplish something marvelous. Joseph realizes this only in retrospect. By looking back he can see the pattern of God's providence in his life and that of his brothers as well. God intended it for good—not only the good of Joseph and his brothers, but the good of the whole world. Through the survival of Joseph's family an entire nation would emerge, and from this nation the Messiah would be born.

3. God uses suffering and tragedy as occasions to display his glory. In the face of suffering and tragedy, either we can deny God's ability to prevent the disaster, and consequently think of God as impotent in the face of radical evil, or, more commonly, we can blame God for not intervening. When a fellow minister lost his young daughter to cancer, a well-known pastor tried to comfort him by saying, "God will have a lot to give account for in heaven." No one can deny these feelings when faced with such a crisis. The Bible itself, especially the Psalms, overflows with questions born of pain and doubt. "How long, O LORD?" "Why is your mercy gone forever?" "Why do the evil triumph and the righteous suffer?" But true piety knows that, behind the suffering, we experience the one God who ever remains in his justice, a wise and loving Father who has promised never to leave or forsake us. When we charge God with complicity in evil, we assume that God and humans are subject to the same standards of judgment. That's like comparing apples and oranges, or asking how many inches are in a pound. What God said through the prophet Isaiah still stands:

> For my thoughts are not your thoughts,
>
> > neither are your ways my ways, declares the LORD.
>
> For as the heavens are higher than the earth,
>
> > so are my ways higher than your ways
> >
> > and my thoughts than your thoughts. (Isa. 55:8–9)

The Bible spends little time answering the whys and wherefores of life. Rather, it tells us that "the secret things belong to the LORD our God, but the things that are revealed belong to us and to our children forever" (Deut. 29:29). When confronted with a man born blind (see John 9), Jesus refused to talk about the cause of his blindness. He does say that the blindness was *not* caused by his own sin or his parents' sin. Jesus focused not on causation, but on purpose: this happened "that the works of God might be displayed in him" (John 9:3). His blindness became the occasion for God's grace as God healed him physically and spiritually, and he became an effective witness to the saving power of Christ.

4. God's grace is sufficient when the answer is no. Second Corinthians 12:7–10 is one of the most important passages in the Bible on the role of providence in the Christian life. Paul tells us that he had a debilitating physical ailment, "a thorn in the flesh." We do not know what this "thorn" meant (some have guessed blindness or epilepsy), but Paul tells us four important things about it. First, God "gave" it to him for his spiritual well-being—to keep him from arrogance and pride. Second, the Devil had a hand in it: Paul was tormented by "a messenger of Satan." This recalls the way God allowed Satan to afflict

Job in the Old Testament. Third, Paul repeatedly prayed for relief, but God answered him with no. Finally, through this experience Paul drew closer to Christ. He came to know more deeply the sufficiency of God's grace. At the end of the experience he said: "Now I take limitations in stride, and with good cheer, these limitations that cut me down to size—abuse, accidents, opposition, bad breaks. I just let Christ take over! And so the weaker I get, the stronger I become" (2 Cor. 12:10, MESSAGE).

I shall never forget Sue McIntyre. She was the wife of the pastor who ordained me to the gospel ministry, Dr. J. Ralph McIntyre. Sue was one of the godliest women I have ever known. She radiated the love of Jesus in everything she ever did. She was a great encouragement to me and to the other young people in the church. Soon after I moved to Boston to begin graduate studies, I learned that Sue had been diagnosed with cancer. She struggled for several years but then died in the prime of life. I was not able to go home for the funeral, but someone sent me a tape of the service. I remember listening to the voice of her husband as he delivered the message at her funeral. He said that if he could snap his fingers and change the course of events, he would do so in a second for he loved his "sweet Sue" (as he called her). But then he went on to say that he was not angry with God over what had happened. He and Sue had talked together before she died. Even though they had many questions neither one could answer, they both found God's grace completely sufficient for the valley they were walking through together. And this has been the testimony of countless Christians through the ages:

> When all around, my soul gives way,
> He then is all my hope and stay.[10]

5. *The cross is the place where grace and providence embrace.*
Where can we look to find confirmation of Romans 8:28, to know

that God's work of grace will finally triumph over all obstacles? We can see some evidence of this in our own lives, especially as we review them retrospectively through the lenses of God's redemptive love. Sometimes we can see what appears to be God's movement on a grand scale in history, as with the fall of Communism in Russia and the Soviet bloc a generation ago. But these perspectives are always partial, incomplete. We are still looking into a mirror with blurred vision.

We can look one place, however, and know beyond all doubt that Romans 8:28 is true: the cross of our Lord Jesus Christ. We call it Good Friday, but it proved to be one of the darkest days in history. Abandoned by his followers and friends, a crucified Jesus experienced a God-forsaken death for God-forsaken sinners. Amazingly, when Christians looked back on this event, they saw not defeat but triumph, for God was in Christ reconciling the world unto himself on that cross. Thus in an ancient Syrian liturgy, the early Christians sang, "The Lord hath reigned from the tree."[11] God used the innocent, shameful, despicable suffering of his own Son to bring about the eternal good of redemption. We can be sure he will also take the shards and broken fragments in our lives and piece them together into a mosaic of beauty and wonder. The God who neither slumbers nor sleeps will see us through the darkest night and bring us safe at last to that blessed place where we will need neither lamp nor light of sun. God himself will be our radiance. What a great comfort amid the slings and arrows of outrageous fortune! What a great God of majesty and wonder, worthy of worship and praise, as Isaac Watts knew when he wrote this hymn:

> Tell of His wondrous faithfulness,
> And sound His power abroad;
> Sing the sweet promise of His grace,
> And the performing God.

The Providence Mystery

Engraved as in eternal brass,
The mighty promise shines;
Nor can the powers of darkness rase
Those everlasting lines.

His very word of grace is strong
As that which built the skies;
The voice that rolls the stars along
Speaks all the promises.[12]

Three

Saved by Grace

On our feet we may have arguments,
but on our knees we are all agreed.[1] ~ J. I. PACKER

Recently I received a package of special ginseng-flavored tea as a present. As I opened the box, I noticed the following verse, entitled "Determination," inscribed on the back:

Gifts count for nothing; will alone is great;
All things give way before it, soon or late. . . .
Each well-born soul must win what it deserves.
     . . . The fortunate
   Is he whose earnest purpose never swerves,
   Whose slightest action or inaction serves
The one great aim.
       Why, even Death stands still,
And waits an hour sometimes for such a will.[2]

Since Adam and Eve fell in the garden of Eden, the following senti-ments have been the creed of graceless human beings. Gifts count for nothing. What counts is your will, your determination. You can make it on your own. Grace is for weaklings. You need no Savior to die for you. You can save yourself by what you do and how you live. Just dig in deeper, and try harder! William Ernest Henley's famous poem, "Invictus," expresses the same idea in its exaltation of

> . . . my unconquerable soul. . . .
> I am the master of my fate;
> I am the captain of my soul.[3]

Yet anyone who has been truly born again knows that this cannot be right. Self-salvation is an utter impossibility. Life itself is a gift. Moment by moment we are sustained by God's gracious providence. Everything we are and have is the result of our absolute dependence on God's mercy. Sometimes, though, we have to be brought low before we realize this basic truth. Jonah had spent some time in the belly of the great fish before he was ready to confess, "Salvation is of the LORD" (Jonah 2:9, KJV).

Occasionally when I am speaking at a church or a Bible conference, some young person will ask me to sign his or her Bible. When I do, I always include a reference to my favorite Bible verse, 1 Corinthians 4:7. This verse shatters the myth of self-reliance and points us to the reality of salvation by grace better than any other text I know. It consists of three questions:

1. "Who makes you different from anyone else?"
2. "What do you have that you did not receive?"
3. "And if you did receive it, why do you boast as though you did not?" (NIV)

When they reflect on it, all Christians know that God did not save them because they are better, or smarter, or nicer looking, or even more religious than anyone else. In the Old Testament, God reminded the children of Israel that he had not chosen them because they were large in number, or mighty in battle, or rich in resources. No, they were at the very bottom of "the most favored nation" list. Why, then, did God choose Israel? Because of his unmerited favor. He loved them— just because! And what can any of us claim to have, to possess, that we have not first received as a gift? The honest answer has to be . . . nothing at all. The air we breathe, the clothes we wear, the food we eat, our family, our job, our friends, our faith: all of this has come to us as a gift from our gracious God (see James 1:17). Because this is true, there is no basis for boasting in the Christian life, no room for one-upmanship in the family of God. In the realm of grace, we lose all our bragging rights. Here we can only glory "in the cross of our Lord Jesus Christ" (Gal. 6:14).

The Bible could not be more emphatic that salvation is a free gift of God. As Paul put it, "There is no distinction: for all have sinned and fall short of the glory of God, and are justified by his grace as a gift, through the redemption that is in Christ Jesus" (Rom. 3:22–24). And yet the doctrine of grace has been the subject of continual controversy throughout the history of the church. Why is this? Partly because the grace of God, for all its simplicity, is a difficult teaching to accept. There is a natural resistance to the extravagance of grace. Like the prodigal son returning from the far country, we think we must "do something" to earn the Father's favor. But there is another reason for the controversy as well. Like the mystery of providence, the doctrine of salvation by grace alone raises difficult questions about divine sovereignty and human responsibility, about predestination and the universal love of God. Earnest, Bible-believing Christians have not always seen eye to eye on such matters, and sometimes their quarrels have been noisy and divisive.

In this chapter, we shall review some of the classic debates about grace and look at some of the terms that are often used in this ongoing struggle. We cannot possibly resolve all of these differences in a few pages, but we will seek for better understanding. Where we must in good conscience differ from one another in our interpretation of certain aspects of God's grace, let us do so with love and humility, remembering the words of the great missionary statesman Luther Rice: "Let us not . . . become bitter against those who view this matter [the doctrine of election] in a different light, nor treat them in a supercilious manner; rather let us be gentle towards all men. For who has made us to differ from what we once were? Who has removed the scales from our eyes?"[4]

AUGUSTINE: THE TEACHER OF GRACE

The first great battle over the doctrine of grace in the history of the church took place more than three hundred years after the death of the apostle Paul. This involved a terrific struggle between Augustine (354–430), one of the greatest theologians who ever lived, and Pelagius (b. ca. 354), a British monk and moral reformer who stressed the ability of human beings to make themselves pleasing to God by obeying the law. Later Christians referred to Augustine as *doctor gratiae*, "the teacher of grace," because his influence was so great in this area.

Augustine's theology of grace grew out of his own experience of utter impotence and helplessness before God. In his famous autobiography, *The Confessions*, Augustine described his struggle, and his failure, to live a life pleasing to God:

> From the mud of my fleshly desires . . . belched out murky clouds that obscured and darkened my heart until I could not distinguish the calm light of love from the fog of lust. The two swirled about together and dragged me . . . over the cliffs of my desires, and engulfed me in a whirlpool of sins. . . . I poured myself out, frothed and floundered in the tumultuous sea of my fornications; and you were silent. . . . By your sheer grace and mercy you melted my sins away like ice.[5]

In his search for peace, Augustine tried many religions and many schools of thought. For several years he was a follower of Manichaeism, a fatalistic religion based on radical dualism: light and darkness, good and evil locked forever in a great cosmic battle. Then he became a skeptic. Skepticism was a popular philosophy that denied the possibility of absolute truth. Augustine's conversion to Christ occurred as he was sitting in a garden reading a passage from Romans 13. In this moment he realized that all his self-striving was useless and would never lead him to God. By God's grace he resolved to "put on the Lord Jesus Christ" (v. 14). Immediately, as he says, "the light of certainty flooded my heart and all dark shades of doubt fled away."[6]

Augustine rediscovered what Paul had proclaimed: apart from the grace of Christ we are hopelessly lost and can do nothing to save ourselves. This was the basis of Augustine's prayer, "Oh Lord, give what you command, and command whatever you will." When Pelagius heard this prayer, he was infuriated because it seemed to undercut the moral nerve of the Christian faith. If we are not able to obey God's commandments, then why has he given them in the first place? Salvation, Pelagius said, comes about by the performance of good works and the fulfillment of obligations laid down by God. We can summarize the theology of Pelagius in five propositions, each of which Augustine strongly opposed in the course of the Pelagian controversy.

1. Adam was created mortal; he would have died had he never sinned. This view of death is as popular today as it was in Pelagius's day. How often have you heard death extolled as "a normal part of life," with no intrinsic connection to our moral standing before God? However, Augustine, again following Paul, taught that "the wages of sin is death," physical as well as spiritual (Rom. 6:23). While we cannot correlate personal illness and death with the specific sins of this or that individual, we do live in a fallen world where everything in nature, including our physical bodies, is subject to the laws of decay, corruption, and death. Indeed, as the Bible teaches, the whole creation is "groaning," like a woman about to give birth to a child, as it yearns for the deliverance that Christ will bring at his second coming (see Rom. 8:18–25).

2. *Sin is transmitted by imitation, not by propagation.* For Pelagius, there was no real connection between our sin and Adam's. Adam set us a bad example, to be sure, but that was it. Human beings are born without sin, and they commit sins only by imitating the bad example of others. Augustine, on the other hand, developed a robust doctrine of original sin, the idea that sin is a fundamental condition of estrangement from God. Furthermore, like a hereditary disease, it is passed down from one generation to another.

3. *Grace is not opposed to nature but rather is present within nature.* If Augustine taught original sin, Pelagius believed in original uprightness. We do not need to be "born again," since we were born just fine the first time! If we do sin, we can reform ourselves by strenuous moral effort. Pelagius did concede that God had provided two extra "umphs" of grace after creation, one in the Old Testament, the other in the New: namely, the giving of the law, and the sending of Christ. The law was the perfect rule book, and Jesus was the perfect rule keeper, nothing more. Salvation, like sin, is by imitation too. Augustine, however, realized the futility of this approach. It was like setting an ostrich egg in front of a banty hen and telling her, "Now look at this one, and try harder next time!" The human situation, Augustine claimed, was far more serious than Pelagius allowed. Only a supernatural work of God, which comes to sinners from outside themselves, could make any real difference in their standing before a holy God.

4. Perfection in this life is possible. Pelagius did not say that sinless perfection is easy, nor did he claim to be perfect himself. But he did believe that, in addition to Jesus, there are perfect people who infallibly obey all of God's commands. It is the worst kind of defeatism, he thought, to tell Christians in advance that perfection is unattainable. Augustine held the contrary view. Christians can make great progress in their walk with the Lord, and they should be encouraged to do so. We are called to grow in holiness, but sin is an ever-present reality with which we must struggle until we draw our last breath. Every day we should offer this petition from the Lord's Prayer: "Forgive us our debts" (Matt. 6:12).

5. Predestination is subordinate to foreknowledge. When the Bible speaks of God's predestination of the elect, Pelagius said, it is merely speaking of his ability to see into the future and ratify in advance, so to speak, what he foreknows human beings will do by their own efforts. Augustine, again following Paul, grounded predestination in "God's good pleasure" (see Eph. 1:5). Pelagius saw predestination as God's pretemporal acknowledgment of what human beings through their own merits will do to purchase their own salvation. This interpretation, Augustine countered, allows human beings to become their own savior, or at least their own co-redeemer, in which case they have themselves, and not God, to thank for their salvation—a blasphemous thought!

How does human free agency fit into all of this? In spite of his insistence on the sovereignty of grace, Augustine never understood himself as denying the natural freedom of the will. The term *free will* itself (*liberum arbitrium* in Latin) is not found in the Bible. It is a term the second-century theologian Tertullian, who also coined the word *Trinity*, borrowed for Christian usage from the ancient Stoic philosophers. Augustine, too, spoke frequently of the human "free will" by which he meant the ability of a man or woman to act or decide freely without being compelled or forced by some external constraint. Indeed, one of the first books he wrote as a Christian was entitled *On Free Will*. It was a defense of free moral agency against Manichaean determinism, the religion of fatalism from which he himself had been delivered.

For Augustine, the human will is always moved in one direction or another by the object of its love. In the garden of Eden, Adam and Eve were capable of moving either toward the love of God (*amor Dei*), or away from God and toward the love of self (*amor sui*). When they chose the latter, something disastrous happened both for them and for all their human descendents. Their free will was left intact in the sense that it was still *they* who acted and loved, and *they* who were therefore morally responsible for what they did; however, their free will was so distorted by sin that it was drawn away from the love of God, the true purpose for which they had been created. Now it was pulled in its innermost desires toward the love of self. In other words, human free will was so weakened by sin and the fall that it became "curved in on itself" (*incurvatus in se*). We can illustrate Augustine's conception of human free will before the fall in figure 2.

Fig. 2

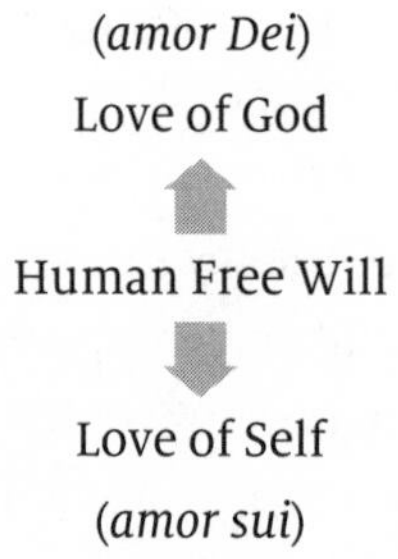

(*amor Dei*)
Love of God

⬆

Human Free Will

⬇

Love of Self
(*amor sui*)

Human free will was not eliminated or destroyed by the fall, but it was so thoroughly contaminated, so filled with pride and self-seeking, that it was now disposed to choose objects of desire that inevitably led it farther and farther away from God. This is what Paul meant, Augustine said, when he declared in Romans 3:10–11,

> None is righteous, no, not one;
>> no one understands;
>> no one seeks for God.
> All have turned aside; together they have become worthless;
>> no one does good,
>> not even one.

Augustine's view of human free will after the fall can be seen in figure 3.

Fig. 3

(*amor Dei*)
Love of God

Human Free Will

Love of Self
(*amor sui*)

This is why Pelagius's advice about "trying harder next time" and picking ourselves up by our own bootstraps is so tragically flawed. Anyone who has suffered from severe drug or alcohol addiction can understand Augustine's point. It is not sufficient to say to such addicts, "Just quit drinking," or "Get off drugs!" Their will has been so misshapen by their addiction that good advice alone is not enough to change their habits. Something must happen to transform them within. Their "want to" must be changed. Augustine believed that all human beings apart from grace are addicts—addicted to sin, pride, and self-centeredness. He knew that we were created by God for fellowship with him, and that our hearts would always be restless until they found true rest in him. But this kind of reorientation requires the operation of divine grace. As Jesus said in John 15:5 (one of Augustine's favorite Bible verses), "Apart from me you can do nothing." From first to last, we are absolutely dependent upon God for our salvation.

Augustine rendered a great service to the gospel in recovering the Pauline theology of grace. Pelagius was an earnest, well-meaning moralist, but his understanding of human nature and salvation was not merely erroneous but heretical. This was recognized at the Council of Ephesus, which condemned his views in 431, one year after Augustine had died. Pelagian ideas still exist today in certain forms of liberal theology, the human potential movement, and even some strands of positive-thinking, "can do" evangelicalism, which stresses self-improvement more than salvation by grace.

The influence of Augustine was great, and later theologians, Protestants and Catholics alike, frequently quoted him in support of their own views. While his understanding of grace was thoroughly biblical, not all of his views were equally sound. For example, he connected the practice of infant baptism to the doctrine of original sin in a way that cannot be justified from the Scriptures. He also believed that the sacraments were necessary channels of God's grace. This led later theologians, such as Thomas Aquinas, to construct an elaborate sacramental theology based on merit and the performance of good works that were seen as necessary conditions for remaining in "a state of grace." In this way, Pelagianism, though officially condemned, re-entered through the back door.

When the printing press was invented in the fifteenth century, Augustine's writings were among the first to be published. The Protestant Reformers, especially Martin Luther, John Calvin, and Thomas Cranmer, were avid readers of Augustine. They discovered in "the teacher of grace" an understanding of salvation that pointed them beyond the abuses of medieval Catholicism and back to the apostolic message of the Scriptures.

THREE DEBATES

The doctrine of grace is like an underground spring of hot water that is always bubbling just below the surface and occasionally bursts forth into a spectacular geyser. Augustine was a great champion of grace, and his views on the subject have influenced all subsequent thinkers. But his teaching has also been qualified and modified in many ways. Each new generation, it seems, must struggle with the issues of grace and human freedom for itself. In the next chapter, we are going to see how our understanding of divine grace relates to other teachings of the Christian faith. But we must first examine three classic debates that continue to shape the way Christians understand these issues.

Luther and Erasmus

Martin Luther (1483–1546) was an Augustinian monk who, amid many struggles, came to a new understanding of God, faith, and the church based on his intensive study of the Holy Scriptures. The heart of Luther's theology was that in Jesus Christ the sovereign God has given himself, utterly and without reserve, for us. The gift of salvation, he said, must be appropriated by faith alone. To have faith is to accept the acceptance that is ours in Jesus Christ. But saving faith is not a self-generated human activity; it is a gift of the Holy Spirit. Luther's great discovery of the gospel became the watchword of the Reformation: *Justification by grace alone, through faith alone, in Jesus Christ alone.*

The Dutch humanist, Desiderius Erasmus (1469–1536) was the greatest scholar of the sixteenth century, and he agreed with Luther's criticism of the abuses in the church. He also edited the first published edition of the Greek New Testament, which Luther used to develop his Reformation theology. Thus some have said, "Erasmus laid the egg that Luther hatched!" In 1524, however, Erasmus published a treatise on the freedom of the will in which he attacked Luther's strong Augustinian understanding of grace. Erasmus was not a pure Pelagian, for he did recognize the necessity of grace. But he underestimated the devastating impact of the fall in tilting human beings away from God. Consequently, he failed to see (what even Thomas Aquinas understood) that it does not lie in the power of sinful human beings to begin the journey to salvation apart from the special intervention of God's grace.

Part of the difficulty arose from Erasmus's definition of free will as the power "by which a man can apply himself to the things which lead to eternal salvation, or turn away from them."[7] This definition confuses the natural capacity of human beings to make non-coerced choices, which Augustine and Luther gladly admit, with that true freedom from sin and death that Paul referred to as "the glorious freedom of the children of God" (Rom. 8:21, NIV). This is the kind of freedom Jesus had in mind when he said: "You will know the truth, and the truth shall set you free" (John 8:32). On the basis of Erasmus's definition, not even the saints in heaven would be free, for there they are not constantly confronted with the "choice" of remaining with God in bliss or joining Satan and the damned in the inferno. But who could imagine that in heaven we will be unfree, deprived somehow of free moral agency? To the contrary, heaven will be the "freest" of all places! There we shall be liberated from the presence of sin as well as from its penalty and power. There for all eternity we shall freely and joyfully worship God and enjoy him forever.

Luther responded to Erasmus's attack in a treatise of his own, *The Bondage of the Will*, published in 1525. In the heat of the argument, Luther used the language of "necessity," and this has led some scholars to accuse him of fatalism. But in speaking of the will's bondage, Luther was merely developing an image originally drawn by Jesus:

"Everyone who commits sin is a slave of sin," and "You are of your father the devil, and your will is to do your father's desires" (John 8:34, 44). God clearly desires that we should be truly free in our love toward him, Luther says, but this is not a possibility until we have been first *freed* from our captivity to Satan and self.

When he tried to square this teaching with the doctrine of predestination, Luther realized that he had entered the realm of mystery. There are, he suggested, three lights—the light of nature, the light of grace, and the light of glory. By the light of grace we are able to understand many problems that appear insoluble by the light of nature, that is, apart from God's special revelation in the Bible. Even so, in the light of glory, God's righteous judgments—incomprehensible to us now even by the light of grace—will be openly manifested. Luther thus appealed to the eschatological vindication of God's plan of redemption in eternity. Ultimately, when we shall have proceeded through the lights of nature and grace into the light of glory, what now seems hidden and mysterious will be openly manifest for all the universe to see (fig. 4).

Fig. 4

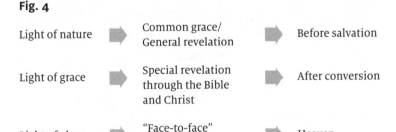

Light of nature	➡	Common grace/General revelation	➡	Before salvation
Light of grace	➡	Special revelation through the Bible and Christ	➡	After conversion
Light of glory	➡	"Face-to-face" relationship with God	➡	Heaven

As a pastor, Luther was often asked to counsel with ordinary Christians who were upset about the dark riddles of grace and election. Typical was his response to Barbara Lisskirchen, who was distressed that she was not among the elect:

When such thoughts assail you, you should learn to ask yourself, "If you please, in which Commandment is it written that I should think about and deal with this matter?" When it appears that there is no such commandment, learn to say, "Begone, wretched devil! You are trying to make me worry about myself. But God declares everywhere that I should let him care for me."

. . . The highest of all God's commands is this, that we should hold up before our eyes the image of his dear Son, our Lord Jesus Christ. Every day he should be our excellent mirror wherein we behold how much God loves us and how well, in his infinite goodness, he has cared for us in that he gave his dear Son for us.

In this way, I say, and in no other, does one learn how to deal properly with the question of predestination. It will be manifest that you believe in Christ. If you believe, then you are called. And if you are called, then you are most certainly predestinated. Do not let this mirror and throne of grace be torn away from before your eyes. . . . Contemplate . . . Christ given for us. Then, God willing, you will feel better.[8]

The mystery of election, Luther teaches us, can be approached only through the cross, through the "wounds of Jesus." It is not a matter for speculation and theological debate. Instead, it is a window into the gracious will of the God who spared not his own Son but freely gave him up for us all.

Calvinists and Arminians

John Calvin (1509–1564) was a second-generation Reformer who took many of Luther's ideas and transplanted them to the city of Geneva, which became the nerve center of international Protestantism. Calvin's ideas radiated out from Switzerland to Hungary and Poland in the East, and to Scotland and the Netherlands in the West. Eventually they were brought to the New World by the Pilgrims and the Puritans.

The greatest theologian of New England was a Calvinist, Jonathan Edwards.

Calvin's name is forever linked with the doctrine of predestination, which he undoubtedly believed and taught in a strict Augustinian form. He did so because he believed this teaching is clearly found in the Scriptures. But he also warned against parading the message of election before novices in the faith. He urged his followers to say no more about predestination than could be derived from the Bible: "We should not investigate what the Lord has left hidden in secret . . . [nor] neglect what he has brought out into the open, so that we may not be convicted of excessive curiosity on the one hand, or of excessive ingratitude on the other."[9] Since God alone knows whom he has elected to salvation, we must preach the gospel to everyone, trusting the Holy Spirit to use it as an effective means for calling to faith those who have been chosen in Christ before the foundation of the world. Predestination, as Calvin understood it, is neither a church steeple from which to view the human landscape nor a soft pillow to sleep on. It is rather a stronghold in times of temptations and trials and a confession of praise to God's grace and to his glory.

Was Calvin himself always faithful to his own advice about not speculating beyond the bounds of revelation? Perhaps not. Later Calvinists certainly seem to have forgotten his words as they became embroiled in endless debates over the ordering of God's decrees, evidences of election in one's activity in the world, the extent of the atonement, and so forth. Theodore Beza, Calvin's successor in Geneva, and William Perkins, a Puritan theologian in England, among others, attempted to recast Calvin's biblical theology in a more systematic, logically rigorous form. For them the doctrine of predestination became the starting point for theology. This was going far beyond Calvin, for whom predestination was a fact of Scripture but not the controlling principle of all Christian doctrine.

In early seventeenth-century Holland, a fierce debate arose over the doctrine of election between strict Calvinists and Arminians (so called from Jacob Arminius, a professor at Leyden University), who sought a looser formulation of Reformed theology. Soon the whole Dutch nation became embroiled in this dispute. Predestination was the topic of discussion in the marketplace as well as in the pulpit. Common people argued about election and the mysteries of grace in towboats and in taverns, from the fish market to the courthouse. The conflict was exacerbated by political and social factors. In 1618–1619 an international assembly of Reformed theologians gathered at the Synod of Dort to resolve the controversy. In response to certain theses put forth by the Arminians (who were also called the Remonstrants), the Synod of Dort outlined the orthodox Calvinist understanding of salvation in terms of five central principles. These are often called "the five points of Calvinism." Because tulips are the national flower of Holland, where the city of Dort is located, these ideas are sometimes arranged in the form of the following acrostic:

T	Total Depravity
U	Unconditional Election
L	Limited Atonement
I	Irresistible Grace
P	Perseverance of the Saints

It is important to point out that this was an intra-Reformed argument. In fact, Arminius himself was much closer in many of his ideas to Calvin than to some latter-day Arminians. Arminius was certainly no Pelagian. Far more than Erasmus, he realized that human free will had been seriously damaged by the fall. He also believed that only as human beings are endowed with faith through the Holy Spirit can they really love God and exercise the freedom for which they were created. For Arminius, however, grace is resistible and the atonement is universal in its scope. Predestination was based on God's fore-knowledge, but not (as Pelagius had supposed) on his foreknowledge of foreseen merits. It was rather God's foreknowledge of foreseen *faith* that conditioned his election of believers. In this way, Arminius held strongly to the Protestant teaching of justification by faith alone while at the same time qualifying the Augustinian-Calvinist doctrine of predestination in a significant way. In the next chapter, we shall revisit the so-called five points of Calvinism. It is important to note that both evangelical Calvinists and evangelical Arminians affirm the reality of God's grace, although they differ among themselves on its implications for other doctrines.

Wesley and Whitefield

Between the death of Arminius in 1609 and the birth of John Wesley in 1703, Arminianism as a system of thought lost much of its evangelical emphasis. Many Arminians became rationalists or deists, denying biblical miracles and the supernatural origins of the Christian faith. Others were drawn into Unitarianism, repudiating both the doctrine of the Trinity and the divinity of Christ. However, not all Arminians followed this path. The Great Awakening of the eighteenth century was led by two anointed servants of God: one a Calvinist, George Whitefield; the other an Arminian, John Wesley.

Whitefield and Wesley were good friends from their student days at Oxford when both were members of the "Holy Club," a nickname given to those who followed a disciplined life of study and prayer. Both men were "savingly converted" in the 1730s and became leaders in the great revival that was sweeping through England. Whitefield made thirteen trips across the Atlantic, bringing the fires of awakening to the American colonies, while Wesley traveled by horseback some 225,000 miles organizing Methodist societies throughout Britain.

Wesley and Whitefield held differing views about the doctrine of predestination, and this led to a strain on their friendship. Wesley once admitted that he was just "a hair's breadth" from Calvinism. He believed strongly in the sovereignty of God, the doctrine of original sin, and the necessity of the new birth. But he could not accept the ideas of unconditional election and irresistible grace. Neither did he believe in the perseverance of the saints. Salvation, once received, could be forfeited, he thought, by falling into serious sin. On all of these issues, Whitefield remained a Calvinist. He also refused to accept Wesley's ideas about sinless perfection.

After many years of disagreement and disputation, both men realized that their differences would not likely be settled this side of heaven. Through the influence of several mutual friends, including Charles Wesley, John's hymn-writing brother, the two great evangelists were reconciled. The theological differences remained, and there was no effort to sweep them under the rug, but they realized that their love for the lost and their common commitment to the gospel far outweighed their disputes about the details of predestination.

Whitefield died on September 30, 1770, in Newburyport, Massachusetts. He had requested that his memorial service in England be conducted by his old friend John Wesley. On this occasion Wesley spoke movingly of Whitefield's many labors for the Lord, his tenderheartedness, his charitable spirit, his loyalty and friendship. He concluded with a question, "Have we read or heard of any person who called so many thousands, so many myriads of sinners to repentance?"[10]

The love and mutual respect Whitefield and Wesley had for one another, despite their strong doctrinal divergence, was an important example for later generations of Christians. During both the First and Second Great Awakenings in America, Baptists, Methodists, Presbyterians, and other evangelical Christians worked together side by side in sharing the good news of salvation through Jesus Christ alone. They also collaborated in the formation of Bible societies, missionary enterprises, and works of charity and benevolence. Wesley and

Whitefield demonstrated that Bible-believing Christians can disagree in love and still stand together as partners in sharing Jesus' love to the lost. The desire for evangelical unity based on the gospel became a guiding principle in the ministry of other leaders with a heart for missions and evangelism, including Charles Haddon Spurgeon, D. L. Moody, and Billy Graham.

PRINCIPLES OF UNITY

Perhaps you wonder how Christians who hold different views about the nature of predestination, or the extent of the atonement, or the ordering of God's decrees can remain in fellowship with one another, much less work together in a common evangelistic effort. First, let me suggest three paths we must *not* take in our quest for this happy result.

1. We do not achieve unity by compromising our convictions. In discussing matters about which Christians differed with one another, Paul said, "Each one should be fully convinced in his own mind. . . . Why do you pass judgment on your brother? Or you, why do you despise your brother? For we will all stand before the judgment seat of God" (Rom. 14:5, 10).

2. We must never seek togetherness for mere prudential reasons. In the same chapter in which Jesus prayed that his disciples might be one, he also asked the Father to sanctify them in the truth (John 17:17, 21). God's inerrant Word is the infallible standard to which we must always appeal in our efforts to understand the things of God more fully.

3. We must never imagine that doctrinal matters are trivial or unimportant. In some circles this slogan is popular: "Missions unites but doctrine divides." This statement has an alluring appeal, but it is basically false for there is no such thing as missions apart from doctrine. We have no message, no gospel apart from "the faith that was once for all delivered to the saints" (Jude 3). A church with no doctrinal moorings, or with shaky theological foundations, will soon be a church with nothing to say to a lost and dying world.

Thinking constructively, how can we work together in a common Christian cause without violating these principles? Consider these suggestions:

- *Make a careful distinction between primary doctrines of the faith, which may not be compromised without betraying the gospel, and secondary issues, which may be important but are not essential for fellowship.* Everything in God's Word is true and important, else it would not be there, but not everything is of equal importance in every respect. Thus Paul, in describing the heart of the gospel, speaks of those matters that are "of first importance" (1 Cor. 15:3). The second coming of Christ, for example, is a cardinal doctrine of the Christian faith. To deny it is to lapse into serious heresy. But earnest, Bible-believing Christians may honestly differ on some of the details of the end times. Local churches and various associations of Christians set forth their distinctive beliefs in confessions of faith. These documents are not infallible artifacts of revelation, but they do identify a consensual interpretation of the Bible within a given community of faith. For this reason, they are very useful in helping Christians to distinguish primary and secondary matters of faith. We must never forget, of course, that all such confessions are accountable to, and revisable in the light of, the Bible itself.
- *When we have theological disagreements with our brothers and sisters in Christ, it is always appropriate for us to pray for*

additional guidance and illumination from the Holy Spirit.
John Robinson, the pastor of the Pilgrim Fathers, once
said to his flock: "The Lord hath yet more truth and light
to break forth out of his Holy Word."[11] The same Spirit
who inspired the Scriptures long ago must be present in
our hearts and minds when we study them today if we
are to understand them aright.

• *Humility, not arrogance, is the proper attitude in all controversies among Christians.* This is an argument not for
proceeding from lack of conviction, but for recognizing
our own limitations and blind spots. The wisest among
us are still learners in the school of faith.

Returning from these general principles to the doctrine of grace
that we have surveyed historically throughout this chapter, we may
take a parting notice of John Wesley by listening in on a conversation
he had with Charles Simeon on December 20, 1784. At this point in
his life, Wesley was already an old man. Whitefield had been dead
for fourteen years, while Wesley still had seven more to live. Simeon,
like Wesley and Whitefield, was a leader of the evangelical revival
in Great Britain. He agreed more with Whitefield than with Wesley
on the doctrines of grace, but he recognized that Wesley was a great
servant of the Lord. He sought to establish a common basis with him
on those theological principles which mattered most to both of them.
This is Simeon's account of his conversation with Wesley:

SIMEON: "Sir, I understand that you are called an Arminian; and
I have been sometimes called a Calvinist; and therefore I suppose we
are to draw daggers. But before I consent to begin the combat, with
your permission I will ask you a few questions. . . . Pray, Sir, do you feel
yourself a depraved creature, so depraved that you would never have
thought of turning to God, if God had not first put it into your heart?"

WESLEY: "Yes, I do indeed."

SIMEON: "And do you utterly despair of recommending yourself to God by anything you can do; and look for salvation solely through the blood and righteousness of Christ?"

WESLEY: "Yes, solely through Christ."

SIMEON: "But, Sir, supposing you were at first saved by Christ, are you now somehow or other to save yourself afterwards by your own works?"

WESLEY: "No, I must be saved by Christ from first to last."

SIMEON: "Allowing, then, that you were first turned by the grace of God, are you not in some way or other to keep yourself by your own power?"

WESLEY: "No."

SIMEON: "What, then, are you to be upheld every hour and every moment by God, as much as an infant in its mother's arms?"

WESLEY: "Yes, altogether."

SIMEON: "And is all your hope in the grace and mercy of God to preserve you unto His heavenly kingdom?"

WESLEY: "Yes, I have no hope but in Him."

SIMEON: "Then, Sir, with your leave I will put up my dagger again; for this is all my Calvinism; this is my election, my justification by faith, my final perseverance: it is in substance all that I hold, and as I hold it; and therefore, if you please, instead of searching out terms and phrases to be a ground of tension between us, we will cordially unite in those things wherein we agree."[12]

Four

A GRACEFUL THEOLOGY

*The Devil again succeeds in laying his cuckoo eggs in a pious nest.
. . . The sulphurous stench of hell is as nothing compared to the evil
odor emitted by divine grace gone putrid.*[1] ~ HELMUT THIELICKE

When you go shopping at the grocery store, do you take time to read the labels on the food you are about to buy? I do. Labels often have important information about the product within—its ingredients, fiber content, fat grams, how many calories per serving, and so forth. More recently, though, I have become skeptical about such labels for I have discovered that they sometimes distort as much as they reveal. Food labels and claims can be very confusing. Becoming a wise shopper means learning how to decipher the labels. There may be hidden ingredients not listed at all, or cancer-causing preservatives not identified as such. Labels can be libels. They can be downright dangerous!

This is also true in human relationships. *Communist, redneck, egghead, liberal, fundamentalist*—all these terms carry negative baggage. They are frequently used in a pejorative manner to dismiss someone we do not like without taking him or her seriously as a person. *Calvinist* and *Arminian*, while historically justifiable when properly defined, can also become labels with which fellow Christians attack and reproach one another. Thus, "He's a Calvinist!" might mean that he is a mean-spirited, pig-headed, hard-nosed bully who never has any fun and doesn't want anybody else to! Conversely, "She's an Arminian!" might mean that she's a weak-kneed, lily-livered, mushy-minded pushover who has no convictions and won't stand up for what's right! If possible, it would be better to eliminate both terms from our vocabulary. However, since this is not a realistic option, at least we ought to be cautious in our use of them. In all relationships, we do well to remember Paul's word of counsel: "So then let us pursue what makes for peace and for mutual upbuilding" (Rom. 14:19).

To clarify matters, we shall do three things in this chapter. First, we shall consider the question, are Baptists Calvinists? Next, we shall look briefly at the so-called five points of Calvinism, which have traditionally been called "the doctrines of grace." And, finally, we shall look at several serious pitfalls to avoid as we seek to understand the Bible's teaching concerning "the manifold grace of God" (1 Pet. 4:10, NKJV).

ARE BAPTISTS CALVINISTS?

Christians of all denominations have wrestled with the mystery of God's sovereignty and human freedom. The Baptist movement as we know it today began in early seventeenth-century England. Those called Baptists shared many things in common, including a strong commitment to biblical authority, salvation by grace through faith in Christ alone, believers' baptism by immersion, and religious liberty. However, by 1650, there were two distinct streams of Baptist life in England: one inclined to Calvinistic views on election (they were called Particular Baptists because they believed that Christ had died for particular persons); the other more in line with Arminian views on this subject (they were called General Baptists from their belief that the atonement was general or universal in scope). By the eighteenth century, both groups suffered from extremist tendencies. Many of the Generals lost their evangelical beliefs and drifted into Unitarianism, while most of the Particulars so emphasized God's sovereignty that they neglected evangelism. As a result of the revival led by Whitefield and Wesley, both groups experienced an evangelical resurgence, and later in the nineteenth century these two streams became united in the Baptist Union of Great Britain. Charles Haddon Spurgeon, perhaps the greatest preacher Baptists have ever known, combined a staunch Calvinistic theology with a strong evangelistic ministry.

Baptists in America debated the same issues. But the influence of the Philadelphia Baptist Confession (first printed by Benjamin Franklin in 1742) and the writings of Baptist theologian Andrew Fuller reinforced the evangelical Calvinism of most mainstream Baptists. In the first decade of the nineteenth century, David Benedict, a Baptist historian from Rhode Island, made an extensive tour of Baptist churches throughout America. He gave the following summary of the Baptist theology he encountered:

> Take this denomination at large, I believe the following will be found a pretty correct statement of their views of doctrine. They hold that man in his natural condition is entirely depraved and sinful; that unless he is born again—changed by grace—or made alive unto God—he cannot be fitted for the communion of saints on earth, nor the enjoyment of God in Heaven; that where God hath begun a good work, he will carry it on to the end; that there is an election of grace—an effectual calling, etc. and that the happiness of the righteous and the misery of the wicked will both be eternal.[2]

With some notable exceptions, such views were typical of Baptists in the North and South until the Civil War, and for several decades thereafter. Baptists strongly rejected the anti-missionary, anti-evangelistic ideas of hyper-Calvinism while they affirmed both human responsibility and the mystery of God's sovereignty in salvation. As late as 1905, F. H. Kerfoot, a systematic theologian in Louisville, could say, "Nearly all Baptists believe what are usually termed the 'doctrines of grace.'"[3] His successor, E. Y. Mullins, disliked the labels *Calvinist* and *Arminian* and sought to transcend the controversy altogether. While retaining much of the content of traditional Reformed theology, he gave it a new casting by restating it in terms of his distinctive theology of experience. Mullins's counterpart in the North, Augustus H. Strong, tried to harmonize Calvinist theology with modern science and philosophy. At Southwestern Seminary in Texas, W. T. Conner, who had studied with both Mullins and Strong, extended their views, seeking to balance a theology of grace with the call to evangelism and missions. One notable exception to this pattern was Dale Moody, who promoted an unabridged Arminianism, even calling into question the eternal security of the believer.

Are Baptists Calvinists? This question does not admit of a simple yes or no answer for, as we have seen, Baptists historically have been all over the map on the Calvinist-Arminian divide. What can be said without dispute, however, is that there is a strong Calvinist or Reformed stream within the Baptist tradition and that this perspective has been held by some of the most notable shapers of Baptist life and thought. Baptists may not agree on how to resolve (the perhaps irresolvable) tension between divine sovereignty and human free agency, but all Bible-believing Baptists will affirm what the Bible clearly teaches—first, God is sovereign: no one is ever saved by anything he or she does, but only and totally by an act of God; second, human beings are not robots but are fully responsible for their response to God. They have a duty to repent and believe the gospel. And Christians also have a duty to share the good news of Jesus with everyone everywhere.

Some critics seem to take a perverse delight when Christians committed to the authority of the Bible are unable to see eye to eye. Nothing pleases the Devil more than when evangelical believers aim their arrows at one another rather than at him! But God's grace should be a cause for celebration, not division. It is a mark of humility to say, "I may be mistaken about this or that detail concerning the decrees of God or the mystery of election. Come, and let's search the Scriptures together." Paige Patterson, a Southern Baptist educator and theologian, has spoken wisely on this matter:

> Baptists are a people who believe the Bible to be the Word of God as their final authority. They teach that salvation is by grace through faith alone and that adult-like faith witnessed by believers' baptism provides a testimony to a watching world. If we believe those things that all fall within the purview of the Baptist faith, then there is plenty of room for all of us in these various emphases that we bring. There's plenty of room under the umbrella for anyone who is anything from a one- to a five-point Calvinist.[4]

FROM TULIPS TO ROSES

Some differences among Christians are substantial and real, while others stem from misunderstanding and miscommunication. To some extent, perhaps, the latter is the case with the so-called five points of Calvinism. As we saw in chapter 3, these theological terms do not come directly from John Calvin. When we lift that historical debate out of context and bring it into our own discussions, the result can be misleading and artificial. The TULIP formulation itself became popular only in the early twentieth century. It would be better if we could stop talking about "points" at all! In a certain sense, there is only one point—the God of grace and glory. In another sense, there are at least sixty-six points, since every book in the Bible sets forth the gospel of grace. However, the doctrines of grace are often presented in terms of these theological ideas, and we should understand what is meant by them.

To clarify these terms, I suggest a different acrostic. Instead of the traditional TULIP, I recommend that we think of ROSES. Instead of total depravity, let's think about radical depravity. Rather than unconditional election, let's posit sovereign election. In the place of limited atonement, let's put singular (or particular) redemption. Irresistible grace becomes overcoming grace, and perseverance of the saints becomes eternal life. Thus:

R	Radical Depravity
O	Overcoming Grace
S	Sovereign Election
E	Eternal Life
S	Singular Redemption

Let's look briefly at each one of these.

Radical Depravity

From Genesis to Revelation, the Bible teaches that human beings are in a mess. We are born rebels, inheriting a corrupted nature from our parents and growing up in an environment tainted by sin. The Bible describes sin in many ways: missing the mark, taking the wrong path, disobeying God's law, being ruled by pride and self-interest. Sin is a universal deformity of human nature and it places men and women everywhere under the certain reign of death and the inescapable wrath of God (see Rom. 3:9–20; Eph. 2:1–3).

But *total depravity* is not the best way to express this doctrinal truth. It suggests that there is no good whatsoever in human beings, that we are always as wicked as we might possibly be. Yet this is not true. As someone has pointed out, not even Adolf Hitler murdered his own mother! The image of God in fallen human beings has been horribly defaced by sin, but it has not been completely destroyed. *Radical depravity* is a better way of saying that we stand justly condemned before the bar of God's righteous judgment and that we can do nothing to save ourselves.

If previous generations sometimes depicted human nature in gloomy, overly pessimistic terms, the trend today is to make light of sin and its devastating effects. Cornelius Plantinga wisely warns us against this:

> For the Christian church (even in its recently popular seeker services) to ignore, euphemize, or otherwise mute the lethal reality of sin is to cut the nerve of the gospel. For the sober truth is that without full disclosure on sin, the gospel of grace becomes impertinent, unnecessary, and finally uninteresting.[5]

In other words, when we belittle sin, we minimize grace. And the contrary is also true: only when we realize the enormity of our sin can we appreciate the inexhaustible abundance of God's mercy and love. As Paul puts it in Romans 5:20, "Where sin increased, grace abounded all the more."

The real question raised by the doctrine of radical depravity is how bad off fallen human beings are apart from grace. Are they merely sick—morally weak—or are they spiritually dead? The Bible says the latter in Ephesians 2:1: "And you were dead in the trespasses and sins in which you once walked, following the course of this world." Obviously, Paul was talking to people who were physically alive and active—they ate, slept, walked, and so forth—but they were so estranged from God that their very lives were marked by death. This is why the Bible describes becoming a Christian as a resurrection, a rising to new life. This spiritual reality is vividly portrayed in Christian baptism: "We were buried therefore with him by baptism into death, in order that, just as Christ was raised from the dead by the glory of the Father, we too might walk in newness of life" (Rom. 6:4).

Overcoming Grace

The term *irresistible grace* is misleading because it seems to suggest that sinners come to God in a mechanical, impersonal way, as a piece of metal is drawn to a magnet. When pressed very far, this image eliminates human free agency and moral responsibility altogether. In the Bible, not only *can* grace be resisted, but it invariably is: Jonah runs away from God; David sins and tries to cover up his transgression; Peter denies Jesus, and so forth. Like wayward sheep, we have all resisted and gone astray (see Isa. 53:6). I like the term *overcoming grace* because it conveys the truth witnessed to by so many Christians: despite their stubbornness and rebellion, they say, God did not give up on them. Like a persistent lover, he kept on wooing until, at last, his persistence won the day. His love and mercy overcame their rebellious resistance. And thus they confess,

> I sought the Lord, and afterward I knew
>> He moved my soul to seek him, seeking me;
> It was not I that found, O Savior true;
>> No, I was found of Thee.[6]

Another term for *overcoming grace* is *effectual calling*. It means simply that God is able to accomplish what he has determined to do in the salvation of lost men and women. Arminians are right to protest the notions of mechanical necessity and impersonal determinism suggested (and sadly sometimes taught) under the banner of *irresistible grace*. God created human beings with free moral agency, and he does not violate this even in the supernatural work of regeneration. Christ does not rudely bludgeon his way into the human heart. He does not abrogate our creaturely freedom. No, he beckons and woos, he pleads and pursues, he waits and wins. As Spurgeon put it in one of his sermons: "With hands loaded with love he stands outside the door of your heart. Is not this good reason for opening the door and letting the heavenly stranger in, when he can bless you with such a vast extent of benediction?" (see Rev. 3:20).[7]

Sovereign Election

What is election? One definition declares that election is "the gracious purpose of God, according to which he regenerates, sanctifies, and glorifies sinners. . . . It is a glorious display of God's sovereign goodness, and is infinitely wise, holy, and unchangeable. It excludes boasting and promotes humility."[8] Election is unconditional in the sense that it is based not upon our decision for God, but rather upon God's decision for us. This is what Paul means in Romans 9:16: "So then it depends not on human will or exertion, but on God, who has mercy." But the adjective *unconditional* can be misleading if it suggests (as some have taken it to mean) that God's election to salvation does not involve a genuine human response or, even worse, that God elects some people irrespective of Jesus' atoning death on the cross. J. I. Packer defines the biblical doctrine of election in this way:

> Before Creation God selected out of the human race, foreseen as fallen, those whom he would redeem, bring to faith, justify, and glorify in and through Jesus Christ (Rom. 8:28–39; Eph. 1:3–14; 2 Thess. 2:13–14; 2 Tim. 1:9–10). This divine choice is an expression of free and sovereign grace, for it is unconstrained and unconditional, not merited by anything in those who are its subjects. God owes sinners no mercy of any kind, only condemnation; so it is a wonder, and matter for endless praise, that he should choose to save any of us; and doubly so when his choice involved the giving of his own Son to suffer as sin-bearer for the elect (Rom. 8:32).[9]

The phrase "foreseen as fallen" in this definition refers to a technical debate in Reformed theology concerning the ordering of God's decrees. Those who hold, as Packer does, that God's decision to predestine some to election presupposes the fall of humanity are known as *infralapsarians*. The alternative view, known as *supralapsarianism*, regards election as prior to the fall. No one should be overly dogmatic about such distinctions for at best we can only draw inferences from the Scriptures on this matter. We should note, however, that the *infralapsarian* view allows for a stronger declaration of human responsibility and thus is more in keeping with the thrust of the entire biblical message.

What about double predestination? Does God elect some for salvation and others for damnation in the same way? Some teachers in the Christian tradition have thought so. The ninth-century monk Gottschalk of Orbais developed a doctrine of "twin predestination" (*gemina praedestinatio*)—the belief that election and reprobation are symmetrical or side-by-side in God's will. This view has been taught by some Calvinist theologians as well. But when the Bible speaks of the reprobate (as it does in Rom. 9:14–24 and 1 Pet. 2:8), it depicts their "hardening" and eventual damnation as the result of their own disobedience and rebellion against God. God passes them by, and gives them over to the sinful desires of their own hearts (see Rom. 1:24–32).

The doctrine of double predestination, as sometimes presented by overly zealous Calvinists, has led many people astray. In one of the Bible's most graphic descriptions of eternal separation from God, Paul reminded the Thessalonians that "God is just" (2 Thess. 1:6, NIV). No lost sinner who ever comes before the judgment bar of God will be able to blame his eternal condemnation on the fact that he was not elected. The grace of God that brings salvation has appeared to all persons, and each will be held responsible for the light he or she has received (see Titus 2:11). Moreover, the fact that God elects some to salvation is not an indication of injustice where others are concerned; it is an indication of grace where anyone is concerned.

In the meantime, no Christian should attempt to identify the reprobate by name, to pick them out of the crowd. The thief on the cross got in just under the wire, and so have many others, though no one is promised a last-minute conversion, and to presume on the grace of God is utter folly. In the final analysis, however, God is the only census taker of heaven. He alone knows the number of the elect. The Good Shepherd alone knows the identities of the sheep that belong to him. He alone calls each one of them by name (see John 10:1–10). The heavenly Father alone knows his adopted children, all those whom he has chosen, called, and justified, and one day will glorify through his Son, Jesus Christ (see Rom. 8:29–30). Thus we should view every person we meet as potentially numbered among the elect, knowing that anyone who repents and turns to Christ in faith may be saved. This conviction should lead us to share the truth of the gospel with every person who crosses our paths.

C. H. Spurgeon once complained that some of his fellow Calvinists seemed to be "half afraid that perhaps some may overstep the bounds of election and get saved who should not be"![10] He gave the following illustration to show the generosity of a truly graceful theology:

> A mouse had lived in a box all its life, and one day crawled up to the edge of it, and looked round on what he could see. Now the box only stood in the lumber room, but the mouse was surprised at its vastness, and exclaimed: "How big the world is!" If some bigots would get out of their box, and only look a little way round them, they would find the realm of grace to be far wider than they dream.[11]

> There will be more in heaven than we expect to see there by a long way.[12]

Eternal Life

The perseverance of the saints (also called *eternal security* or "once saved, always saved") is the one point of Calvinism most contemporary Baptists believe without reservation. Yet these terms can all be misleading for various reasons. To persevere means to persist, to continue, to be steadfast and unrelenting in purpose. When applied to salvation, doesn't this imply that, while we are saved by grace, we are kept by our own strenuous efforts? The Bible, however, attributes the fact that believers continue to abide in Christ to the keeping power of God. As Eugene Peterson translates Paul's statement in Philippians 1:6, "There has never been the slightest doubt in my mind that the God who started this great work in you would keep at it and bring it to a flourishing finish on the very day Christ Jesus appears" (MESSAGE). Nothing could be clearer: salvation is God's work from start to finish!

Similarly, the "once saved, always saved" slogan can be misused when it is taken to mean that one can receive Jesus as Savior without also owning him as Lord. External religious acts such as making a profession of faith or being baptized make no one a Christian. The gospel of "easy believism" is a distortion of the biblical doctrine of perseverance. Of course, true believers can backslide and fall into heinous sin. They sometimes do. When this happens, however, they are plunged into misery, for they are acting contrary to the new nature imparted to them by the Holy Spirit. The Bible says the Holy Spirit is grieved, deeply offended, by sin in the life of a believer (see Eph. 4:30). Anyone who can sin blithely, flagrantly, flippantly with no sense of uneasiness, no qualms of conscience, is most likely a person who has never been genuinely born again in the first place. One of the marks of being a true Christian is the experience of receiving the loving discipline and chastening from the heavenly Father (see Heb. 12:4–11).

Eternal life is not only life that lasts eternally; it is the very life of God! It can never be extinguished any more than God himself can commit suicide. Jesus, the Good Shepherd, has given his word that those whom the Father has given him will never perish. Instead they will be preserved to glory through all the toils and snares of their earthly journey (see John 10:28–29). Jesus himself is the guarantee of our salvation.

Arminians believe that it is possible for those who have been truly born again to forfeit their salvation through radical disobedience and apostasy. They cite passages such as Hebrews 6:1–6, which can be read to support their view. On closer examination, however, this and other warning passages in the Bible are better applied to those who make a false profession of faith without being truly regenerated. Evidently Peter had this possibility in mind when he encouraged his readers "to make your calling and election sure, for if you practice these qualities you will never fall. For in this way there will be richly provided for you an entrance into the eternal kingdom of our Lord and Savior Jesus Christ" (2 Pet. 1:10–11).

Arminians have another objection to this doctrine too: they think it implies the negation of human free will. If we can resist and reject the call of Christ before conversion, then why not afterward? Are we less free after salvation than before? If God so keeps us that we can neither utterly nor finally fall away from his grace, doesn't this mean that he violates our human freedom?

The difficulty here is twofold. The first is the error Erasmus made in his debate with Luther when he confused the natural freedom of the will (better called *free moral agency*) with freedom from the penalty and power of sin. The latter can come about only through the new birth, whereas the former is part of what it means to be a human being regardless of one's spiritual condition. Second, there is the failure to see that election, as well as perseverance, "comprehends all the means in connection with the end."[13] It is *we* who repent, *we* who believe, and *we* who persevere to the end, although we cannot do any of this on our own. We have our gracious God alone to thank for it all from first to last.

Singular Redemption

Of the five points of Calvinism, limited atonement or singular/particular redemption is the one that is most controversial, and also the one that is least prominent in the Scriptures. As we have seen already, *limited atonement* is a most misleading term for it suggests that there is some deficiency, something missing or lacking, in Christ's work on the cross. But Christ's death is of infinite value. It is fully sufficient to save everyone who ever lived in the entire history of the world. We may even be so bold to declare that Christ's all-sufficient redeeming work would cover any other worlds inhabited by lost souls that astronomers may discover in the future.

Since the Middle Ages, many theologians, including Thomas Aquinas and John Calvin, have made this distinction: Jesus' death is *sufficient* to save all, but it is *efficient* to save only those who repent and believe the gospel. Thus the Reformed position is better described as *definite atonement* or *singular redemption*—singular in the sense of having to do with particular individuals, not just with a general class or group of people. Charles Wesley, whose Arminianism was more moderate than that of his brother John, wrote a beautiful hymn describing the meaning of particular redemption in this sense:

> And can it be that I should gain
> An int'rest in the Savior's blood?
> Died He for me, who caused His pain?
> For me, who Him to death pursued?
> Amazing love! How can it be
> That Thou, my God, shouldst die for me?[14]

The issue of the extent of the atonement is more urgent for those who believe in the penal, substitutionary atonement of Christ. The question then becomes, Did Jesus pay for the sins of the entire human race, or only for those whom he knew the Father would give him to be his own people? Those who believe in particular redemption find support for their view in verses such as Acts 20:28, where Paul speaks of "the church of God, which he obtained with his own blood," and Ephesians 5:25, where we are told that "Christ loved the church and gave himself up *for her*." Again, in Romans 8:33–34, Paul seems to connect election and Christ's intercession as part of a unified nexus of redemption: "Who shall bring any charge against God's elect? It is God who justifies. Who is to condemn? Christ Jesus is the one who died—more than that, who was raised—who is at the right hand of God, who indeed is interceding for us." Again, in John 17:9, Jesus states that he is praying not for the world but rather for those whom the Father had given him, and for others who would believe on him through their witness. Clearly Jesus did not here pray for everyone. In what sense did Jesus die for those for whom he deliberately refused to pray? Further, if he fully paid for the sins of all those who perish eternally, then why are they punished? Would God be just to require them to suffer forever in hell when Jesus has already experienced hell for them, canceling their sin debt on the cross?

These are difficult questions, but those who believe in general redemption or unlimited atonement can cite numerous Scripture passages of their own that declare that Christ did die for the whole world. The message of John the Baptist echoes throughout the New Testament: "Behold, the Lamb of God, who takes away the sin of the *world*!" (John 1:29; see also 2 Cor. 5:19; 1 Tim. 2:6; Heb. 2:9; 1 John 2:2). Moreover, Peter speaks of false teachers and heretics who were "denying the Master who bought them, bringing upon themselves swift destruction" (2 Pet. 2:1). These and other texts seem to indicate that *in some sense* the death of Christ is applicable to all persons without exception, including even those who will ultimately be numbered among the reprobate. The standard Calvinist response to the "all" verses is to say that they refer to all sorts or kinds of people: to princes as well as paupers, to city dwellers as well as country folk, to Africans no less than Asians, and so forth. But this is a strained exegesis that is hard to justify in every case. Unless the context clearly requires a different interpretation, it is better to say that "all means all," even if we cannot square the universal reach of Christ's atoning death with its singular focus.

However one resolves these theological and exegetical difficulties, we should not make one's views on the extent of the atonement a test of doctrinal orthodoxy. The great Texas Baptist leader B. H. Carroll was a consistent Calvinist in his doctrine of election, but he refused to be dogmatic about particular redemption. "Pure verbal realities," Tom Nettles explains, "led him to protect the mysteries of the atonement, in which he saw universal benefits beyond the closures of our systems and even our present comprehension."[15] C. H. Spurgeon affirmed the doctrine of definite atonement, but he also believed, with evangelical Calvinists before and since, that "whosoever will" may come to Christ for salvation. He presented the free offer of the gospel to lost men and women with persistence and passion, and so should we:

Tell me, then, sir, whom did Christ die for? Will you answer me a question or two, and I will tell you whether He died for *you*. Do you want a Saviour? Do you feel that you need a Saviour? Are you this morning conscious of sin? Has the Holy Spirit taught you that you are lost? Then Christ died for you and you will be saved. Are you this morning conscious that you have no hope in the world but Christ? Do you feel that you of yourself cannot offer an atonement that can satisfy God's justice? Have you given up all confidence in yourselves? And can you say with your bended knees, "Lord, save, or I perish"? Christ died for you. . . . Are you a sinner? That felt, that known, that professed, you are now invited to believe that Jesus Christ died for you, because you are a sinner; and you are bidden to cast yourself upon this great immovable rock, and find eternal security in the Lord Jesus Christ.[16]

FALLING FROM GRACE

Before we leave our review of the doctrines of grace, we need to pause and consider how easy it is for the message of grace to be perverted. This has been a problem since the earliest days of Christianity, and it remains so today. Paul's letter to the Galatians was written as a wake-up call to a group of believers who were being tempted to forsake the evangelical message Paul had proclaimed in favor of "a different gospel," a message that mingled the grace of Christ with a theology of works-righteousness. Paul laments the fact that these believers have been alienated from Christ. "You have fallen away from grace," he wrote (Gal. 5:4). This is a favorite prooftext for those who teach that salvation can be forfeited by a truly regenerated believer. But this was not the issue that concerned Paul in this text. He was writing to Christian churches that had been founded on the teaching of grace but that were in danger of forsaking that sound doctrinal bedrock for a theology that could only lead to ruin. It is still possible for Christians to fall from grace in this sense today. Let us look at two ways in which this can happen.

The Labyrinth of Legalism

Labyrinth is a term that comes from ancient Greek mythology. According to legend, King Minos of Crete asked his architect to design an intricate structure with many winding passages and dead ends where he could put the Minotaur, a monstrous animal, half bull and half human. The labyrinth became a perfect prison. There was no escape. One could go forever along its twisting paths without ever finding the exit. And so it is with legalism. Legalism is a distortion of the gospel that robs Christians of the freedom we have in Christ. It subverts the grace of God by taking us back into the captivity of the law. It takes our eyes off Jesus and focuses them on ourselves, filling us with pride. In the labyrinth of legalism we get lost in the maze of our own self-righteousness.

There are two kinds of legalism against which Christians must always be on guard. The first is what I call "the Jesus-*and* heresy." It happens whenever we add anything to Jesus' finished work on the cross as a necessary condition for salvation. In Galatia, Paul's opponents preached a "Jesus-and-circumcision gospel." But this kind of legalism assumes many forms: Jesus and water baptism, Jesus and good works, Jesus and paying our tithes, Jesus and Buddha, Jesus and the Blessed Virgin Mary, Jesus and *anything*! However you interpret the details of the doctrines of grace, they all underscore the fundamental fact of Christianity: salvation is of the Lord, and God will brook no rivals in the dispensing of his grace. Abraham Booth was a Baptist pastor who lived in England some two hundred years ago. In his book *The Reign of Grace* he wrote:

> Divine grace disdains to be assisted in the performance of that work which peculiarly belongs to itself. . . . Attempts to complete what grace begins betray our pride and offend the Lord; but cannot promote our spiritual interest. Let the reader, therefore, carefully remember that grace is either absolutely free, or it is not at all: and, that he who professes to look for salvation by grace, either believes in his heart to be saved entirely by it, or he acts inconsistently in affairs of the greatest importance.[17]

There is also another form of legalism that robs Christians of joy in their walk with the Lord. I call it "the dos-and-don'ts syndrome." This kind of legalism turns Christianity into a gloomy killjoy religion based on the strict observance of an external code of behavior, a pattern of expectations derived more from a particular culture than from the Bible itself. I grew up with this kind of legalistic Christianity. In the church of my childhood, we were quite proud of our separation from the world—from everything that even smelled worldly to us. We looked down on other Christians who dressed differently than we did, who had televisions in their homes, who sang from a different hymnal in church, whose pastor did not perspire in the pulpit as much as ours! Our pastor always removed his suit jacket when he preached. To preach with your coat on was a surefire sign of worldliness, if not liberalism! We were right to be concerned with holy living and a distinctive Christian lifestyle. But we were wrong to make ourselves the standard for all other believers. As a result, we became stodgy and inhibited in our Christian walk. Of course, we believed devoutly that salvation is by grace alone, but our lives betrayed the truth of the doctrine we professed. We were lost in the labyrinth of legalism.

The Abuse of Liberty

The grace of God can be perverted in another way as well: by presuming upon it. The classic name for this attitude is *antinomianism* (from the Greek *anti*, "against," and *nomos*, "law"). Paul encountered this attitude in his day. There were some Christians who argued like this: Since God's grace is absolutely free and unconditional, it doesn't really matter how we live. We love to sin. God loves to forgive. So let's just go on sinning to our heart's content, knowing all the while that God's grace will always be available to cover our misdeeds. Paul was shocked at the way these believers (if indeed they were true Christians!) were abusing their liberty in Christ. He exclaimed, "What shall we say then? Are we to continue in sin that grace may abound? By no means! How can we who died to sin still live in it?" (Rom. 6:1–2).

Behind this dispute lies an important question: Does the law of God have any continuing relevance for Christians after they have been saved? We must never forget that through the redemption secured by Christ's death on the cross, believers have been liberated *from* the law. They have been accepted as righteous before God quite *apart from* the law. Legalism ignores the liberating force of this great truth. But antinomianism is another, equally dangerous, deviation from the truth of the gospel. It reduces the message of salvation to cheap grace. The liberty we have in Christ is not only a freedom *from* but also a freedom *for*—freedom for service and love. As Paul puts it in Galatians 5:1, "For freedom Christ has set us free." Our liberty in Christ is not a static thing, something to be admired and stroked like Silas Marner polishing his gold coins. No, true freedom is realized only through the worship and adoration of God and in selfless love for everyone created in God's image—our neighbors, coworkers, friends, family.

In this sense, the New Testament Christian, as well as the Old Testament saint, can delight in the law of God in accordance with the new nature imparted by grace alone.

> Oh how I love your law!
>> It is my meditation all the day. (Ps. 119:97)

We must never forget that not only are we saved by grace, but we live by grace too. It is only because "God's love has been poured into our hearts" by the Holy Spirit that we are enabled to love God and to love our neighbor as well (Rom. 5:5). The Scottish preacher Ralph Erskine rightly expressed the true relationship of law and gospel in this verse:

> When once the fiery law of God
> Has chas'd me to the gospel-road;
> Then back unto the holy law
> Most kindly gospel-grace will draw. . . .

A Graceful Theology

The law most perfect still remains,
And ev'ry duty full contains:
The gospel its perfection speaks,
And therefore gives whate'er it seeks. . . .

A rigid master was the law,
Demanding brick, denying straw;
But when with gospel-tongue it sings
It bids me fly, and gives me wings.[18]

Five

GRACE AND THE GREAT COMMISSION

The first thing that happens after we have realized our election to God in Christ Jesus is the destruction of our prejudices and our parochial notions. The first thing God will do with us is to pour through the channels of a single heart the interests of the whole world.[1] ~ OSWALD CHAMBERS

In 1970, the Fellowship Baptist Church of Chickamauga, Georgia, called me to be their pastor. Chickamauga was a small mill town in northern Georgia, and this was my first church. I soon learned that Baptists were people of fight as well as faith! We had some terrific battles during my two-year ministry there. Should we buy a church bus? What color should it be painted? Should a carpet be installed in the sanctuary? What about padded pews? Could we put a Ping-Pong table in the fellowship hall so that the young people would have some recreation, or would this desecrate the house of God? We fought over all these issues, but the one I remember most vividly concerned the name of the church.

This became an issue after we had decided to put a sign out front with the church name on it. Brother Walker, one of our elderly deacons, insisted that the sign read "Fellowship *Missionary* Baptist Church." Everybody knew we believed in missions, but why put it on the sign? Brother Walker had moved to northern Georgia from eastern Tennessee, where it was more common for churches committed to the Great Commission to include the word *missionary* in their church name. He remembered debates with some "Primitive" or "hard-shell" Baptists who were opposed to missions—at home or abroad. He didn't want us to repeat the error of those anti-missionary Baptists, and he got his way with the sign.

The attitude Brother Walker encountered as a young boy in eastern Tennessee is sometimes called hyper-Calvinism. In the nineteenth century, it was a powerful movement that ripped across the Baptist landscape, leaving deep scars on many churches and associations. It is one reason why many Baptists (and other Christians too) still fear anything that smacks even slightly of Calvinism. They connect it with the memory of a movement that opposed evangelism and missions, as well as Sunday schools, theological seminaries, orphanages, and cooperative works of any kind. Although this movement no longer persists as an organized threat, some of the attitudes it fostered have not completely died out. As we have seen, Baptists and other evangelical believers often differ among themselves on some of the details of the doctrines of grace. But no one who takes seriously the words of Jesus can ignore his clear command to "go therefore and make disciples of all nations" (Matt. 28:19). Baptists are Great Commission Christians!

In this chapter, we shall look briefly at the anti-missionary movement in Baptist life. We shall then profile two great Baptist heroes of the past, William Carey and Charles Haddon Spurgeon. God used both of these men to deliver Baptists (and other Christians too) from the clutches of a dismal self-focused theology in their own day. They still have much to teach us now.

THE QUAGMIRE OF HYPER-CALVINISM

As we have seen throughout this study, it is possible to get out of theological balance by overemphasizing either the human role in conversion or the divine initiative in salvation. Arminians have sometimes been guilty of the former. Their theology obscures the real meaning of grace and reduces God to a puppet on a string. Hyper-Calvinists have frequently fallen into the opposite error, so exalting God's sovereignty that human responsibility and free moral agency are denied. *Christians must ever be on guard against both extremes!* Either one is deadly to the purpose of evangelism and missions.

A recent Baptist confession of faith states:

> It is the duty and privilege of every follower of Christ and of every church of the Lord Jesus Christ to endeavor to make disciples of all nations. The new birth of man's spirit by God's Holy Spirit means the birth of love for others. Missionary effort on the part of all rests thus upon a spiritual necessity of the regenerate life, and is expressly and repeatedly commanded in the teachings of Christ. It is the duty of every child of God to seek constantly to win the lost to Christ by personal effort and by all other methods in harmony with the gospel of Christ.[2]

Hyper-Calvinists depart from the heart of the evangelical faith in several respects. Here are five of them:

1. They teach the doctrine of eternal justification. All Calvinists believe in election—that from eternity God freely chooses in Christ those who will spend eternity with him in heaven, and that he predestines them "for adoption as sons through Jesus Christ" (Eph. 1:5). But hyper-Calvinism goes beyond this by also pushing justification back into the decrees of God. This teaching seems to remove completely a genuine human response from the process of salvation. Repentance and faith thus lose their urgency, if not their necessity. The Philadelphia Confession of Faith, while strongly affirming the doctrine of election, states clearly that the chosen ones "are not justified personally, until the Holy Spirit doth in due time actually apply Christ unto them."[3] This is much more in keeping with how the Bible describes the relationship between election and justification.

2. They deny the free moral agency and responsibility of sinners to repent and believe. Put otherwise, they confuse radical depravity with natural inability. This implies a deterministic view of human nature that is no different from fatalism. A proper understanding of human responsibility is essential to biblical evangelism. The wrath of God will not be poured out on anyone simply because he or she is one of the non-elect. Instead, people will be justly punished for their sin and rejection of God.

3. They restrict the gospel invitation to the elect. Hyper-Calvinism teaches that since preaching is the means for the ingathering of the elect, it is wrong to preach the gospel indiscriminately to all. This view contradicts the Scriptures in which the gospel is presented as good news for all persons everywhere: "Whosoever shall call on the name of the Lord shall be saved" (Rom. 10:13, KJV). Preachers do not come equipped with some sort of spiritual Geiger counter enabling them to determine who is elect and who is not. As the conversion of the thief on the cross shows, there is no sinner so vile, no one so far gone, but that he or she may be saved by turning to Christ in repentance and faith. The gospel invitation is universal in scope: "Whosoever will, let him take the water of life freely" (Rev. 22:17, KJV).

4. They teach that sinners have no warrant to believe in Christ until they feel the evidence of the Spirit's moving in their hearts. The problem with this view is that it forces lost persons to look to themselves, rather than to Christ, to find the proper basis for becoming a Christian. Although hyper-Calvinism usually errs on the side of utter objectivism, ignoring human responsibility, here ironically it plunges into the abyss of extreme subjectivity. How can lost sinners ever know whether what they are feeling is the genuine moving of the Spirit, or something else? The Bible does not say, "Wait for feelings," but rather, "Trust in Jesus."

5. They deny the universal love of God. We must never deny the holiness and justice of God, which are constitutive of his divine character, but it is the love of God that draws the lost to salvation. It is wrong to play these divine attributes off against one another, for they are perfectly reconciled in the one true God, who is perfect in every way. But let us never forget that God does not love us because Jesus died for us; rather Jesus died for us because God loves us. Jesus loved Jerusalem and wept over it. Paul was compelled by the love of Christ to preach the gospel to everyone he met. The psalmist declares: "How excellent is thy lovingkindness, O God! *therefore* the children of men put their trust under the shadow of thy wings" (Ps. 36:7, KJV).

Hyper-Calvinism, then, is a perversion of true evangelical Calvinism, just as Pelagianism is a corruption of true evangelical Arminianism. In different ways, both are guilty of "falling from grace" in the sense that Paul used that expression in Galatians 5. God wants all believers to be "missionary" Christians, whether we put that name on our church signs or not. Before we turn to Carey and Spurgeon, let's listen to Iain H. Murray, whose study of hyper-Calvinism is one of the best to be published in recent years:

The final conclusion has to be that when Calvinism ceases to be evangelistic, when it becomes more concerned with theory than with the salvation of men and women, when acceptance of doctrines seems to become more important than acceptance of Christ, then it is a system going to seed and it will invariably lose its attractive power.[4]

INTO ALL THE WORLD: CAREY'S BREAKTHROUGH

The man whom we remember today as the father of modern missions, William Carey, was born in a tiny village in England in 1761. He was brought up in poverty and obscurity, with no more than a fifth- or sixth-grade education. Yet he was a genius at mastering languages and translated the Bible into Bengali, Hindi, Sanskrit, and many other languages of India and the East. A sickly boy, he became a shoemaker by trade because he was not able to work outdoors in the sun. He was led to Christ by a fellow apprentice in the shoe shop and baptized as a believer in the river Nene in 1783.

As the young pastor of a village church, he sought to win his family and friends to Christ. But he also had a vision for carrying the gospel into all of the world. This was not a popular idea in Carey's day, even among many Christians who were otherwise quite orthodox in theology. Some were in the grips of the kind of hyper-Calvinistic theology we have just reviewed. They were against human exertions of any kind in the spread of the gospel. Others held that the missionary mandate of the Great Commission was no longer applicable—it applied to the original apostles only! Since the world had already heard the gospel in the apostolic age, they reasoned, what need was there to offer it again? So pervasive was this thinking that it was reflected in an anti-missionary hymn that made the rounds in the eighteenth century:

Go ye into all the world,
The Lord of old did say,

But now where He has planted thee,

There thou shouldst stay.[5]

Their philosophy was simple: Just bloom where you are planted! Don't worry about those who have never heard the good news. Carey rejected this interpretation as a perversion of Jesus' command. There is no statute of limitations on the Great Commission, he said. "Go *ye*" means you and I—and it means here and now!

One of the most famous incidents in Carey's ministry occurred at a meeting of ministers at Northampton. The meeting was moderated by a venerable pastor, John Ryland Sr. He called upon his colleagues to propose a topic for discussion. After an awkward silence, Carey rose and proposed for consideration "the duty of Christians to attempt the spread of the gospel among heathen nations." Ryland was genuinely astonished and, with a rebuking frown, thundered back, "Young man, sit down. When God pleases to convert the heathen, he will do it without your aid or mine!" A later tradition says that he referred to Carey as a "miserable enthusiast" for even raising the issue.[6]

But Carey found an able ally in his good friend and fellow pastor Andrew Fuller. Fuller agreed with Carey completely, and in 1785 he published a masterful defense of missions. His book was called *The Gospel Worthy of All Acceptation*. It contained the following six propositions:

1. Unconverted sinners are commanded, exhorted, and invited to believe in Christ for salvation.
2. Everyone is bound to receive what God reveals.
3. The gospel, though a message of pure grace, requires the obedient response of faith.
4. The lack of faith is a heinous sin, which is ascribed in the Scriptures to human depravity.

5. God has threatened and inflicted the most awful punish-
ments on sinners for their not believing on the Lord Jesus
Christ.

6. The Bible requires of all persons certain spiritual exercises
which are represented as their duty. These include repentance and faith no less than the requirement to love God,
fear God, and glorify God. That no one can accomplish
these things apart from the bestowal of the Holy Spirit is
clear. Nonetheless, the obligation remains. In this respect
"man's duty and God's gift" are the same thing, seen from
different perspectives.[7]

Carey was to develop his missionary theology out of these basic
insights. If sinners were *obliged* to repent and believe in Christ, as
the Bible makes clear, was there not also another obligation to be
considered? Were not Christians, themselves delivered from darkness into light, most urgently *obliged* to present the claims of Christ
to those who have never heard? One of his friends, Robert Hall, put
it this way: "The way to Jesus is graciously open for everyone who
chooses to come to him."[8]

Carey and Fuller were attacked from both the left and the right,
by Arminians and hyper-Calvinists alike. They strongly affirmed the
sovereignty of God in salvation, but far from using this doctrine as
an excuse for a do-nothing approach to missions, Carey and Fuller
called on their fellow Christians to "exert themselves to the utmost"
in fulfilling the Great Commission. The God who predestined the
salvation of the elect, they reasoned, also predestined the means by
which they would be saved. The "means" God had chosen included
the sending of missionaries, the raising up of evangelists, and the
preaching of the gospel in every corner of the world.

In 1792 Carey published his ideas about missions in a little book-
let that became the manifesto of the modern missionary movement.

Its title is worthy of quoting in full: *An Enquiry into the Obligations of Christians, to Use Means for the Conversion of the Heathens, in which the Religious State of the Different Nations of the World, the Success of Former Undertakings, and the Practicability of Further Undertakings, Are Considered*. Carey summed up his plan in four words:

- *Pray*. This is something all Christians can do and ought to do, Carey said. Fervent and united prayer is the divinely appointed prerequisite for a revival of the missionary spirit.
- *Plan*. Carey combined his idealism of absolute commitment with the most practical realism possible. God honors wise planning in missions no less than in any other area of his kingdom's work. Carey the shoemaker never lost his commonsense, no-nonsense approach to missions.
- *Give*. Every Christian has something to offer, Carey said. If all Christians would tithe their income, he observed, there would be an abundance of resources to support the ministry of the gospel at home as well as to sponsor the cause of Christ abroad. There should be special collections, even if it is only one penny per week, and sacrificial giving by all.
- *Go*. Carey volunteered himself. He said to his friends, "I will go down into the mine, if you will hold the ropes."[9] Fuller and a few other friends said they would be the rope holders. They formed the first missionary society and took up the first missionary offering for the express purpose of sending the gospel to those who had never heard the name of Jesus. They were all evangelical Calvinists, and they called their group the "Particular Baptist Society for the Propagation of the Gospel Amongst the Heathen."

And so on June 13, 1793, William Carey, his wife, Dorothy, and their four children, including a nursing infant, sailed from England on a Danish ship headed for India. No one on board that ship would ever see his or her homeland again. Carey served for forty-one years in India without ever coming home on furlough. During those decades, he blazed a trail that thousands of others have followed since then. Carey's missionary legacy is astounding even today: he translated the Scriptures, ran a publishing house, founded a college, organized scores of schools, planted numerous churches, sent out hundreds of Indian evangelists, worked tirelessly for human rights (including the abolition of both slavery and the horrible practice of widow burning), worked for prison reform, and more. What was the secret of his success?

Carey knew that Christian missions was rooted in the gracious, eternal purpose of the triune God—the Father, the Son, and the Holy Spirit—to call unto himself a redeemed people out of the fallen race of humankind. It was not in spite of, but rather because of, his belief in the greatness of God and his divine purpose that Carey was willing to venture all to proclaim the gospel in the far corners of the world. In the midst of great discouragement and even depression, Carey was convinced that God's purpose could not fail. He preached the gospel with compassion but without compromise because he sensed so keenly the eternal destiny of every person he met. He shuddered to think of the dire consequences of spurning Christ's invitation to eternal life.

Time and again Carey was forced to learn the lesson of trusting in God to bring his purpose of love to fulfillment. He entered India as an illegal alien without a passport. He struggled as a farmer to eke out a living for his growing family. There were family tragedies—his young son Peter died; his wife, Dorothy, went mad. There was opposition back home, and some of the "rope holders" let go; there was jealousy from fellow workers and controversy with political leaders. What sustained Carey through all these "toils and snares"? He was resourceful and tenacious, to be sure, but this is not what kept him focused on the goal that had led him to India in the first place. No, his difficulties drove him into the arms of his sovereign Lord. Here he found comfort and strength, as this entry from his diary reveals: "I feel that it is good to commit my soul, my body, and my all, into the hands of God. Then the world appears little, the promises great, and God an all-sufficient portion."[10]

Back in England when Carey was still struggling with the decision to go to India, he visited John Newton, the famous author of "Amazing Grace," who was then a pastor in London. Newton prayed with Carey and offered this counsel: All that is memorable in the annals of history, he said, takes place according to God's plan. Unless God is in this work, all your efforts of utmost strength and wisdom will come to naught. But when God does have a work to accomplish and his time has come, nothing in heaven or upon earth can stand in his way. He is the Lord God almighty, and his works are great and marvelous! To the end of his life, Carey remembered Newton's words. They brought him great comfort and strength when there were few visible results to show for his labors.

Not long before his visit with Newton, Carey had been asked to preach the principal sermon at the annual meeting of his local Baptist association. He took his text from Isaiah 54:2–4:

> Enlarge the place of thy tent, and let them stretch forth the curtains of thine habitations. Spare not, lengthen thy cords, and strengthen thy stakes; for thou shalt break forth on the right hand and on the left; and thy seed shall inherit the Gentiles, and make the desolate cities to be inhabited. Fear not. (KJV)

Carey summarized his message in two simple commands. Together they became the watchword of the modern missionary movement: *"Expect great things from God. Attempt great things for God."*[11]

When kept together and stated in the right order, these two simple imperatives from Carey reflect the right biblical balance between an emphasis on the sovereignty of God and the missionary mandate of the church. Arminianism tends to place the attempting before the expecting. This is to get the cart before the horse: it invariably leads to a prayerless activism that ends in frustrated exhaustion. Hyper-Calvinists, on the other hand, are big on expecting, but they never get around to attempting. They fail to see that the fruit of Christian faith is Christian enterprise, that we are called to be, in the daring language of Paul himself, nothing less than "labourers together with God" (1 Cor. 3:9, KJV). For sure, God is never at our beck and call; but we *are* at his beck and call. Today God still calls us, as he called Carey, to boldness in missions. He wants us to be bold expecters and bold attempters! Looking back on Carey's message, Andrew Fuller had this to say: "I feel the use of his sermon to this day. Let us pray much, hope much, expect much, labor much; an eternal weight of glory awaits us!"[12]

THE GOSPEL FREELY OFFERED TO ALL: SPURGEON'S PASSION

William Carey died in India on June 9, 1834. As he had requested, these words from a hymn by Isaac Watts were inscribed on the stone slab that marked his grave:

A wretched, poor, and helpless worm,
On thy kind arms I fall.[13]

Exactly ten days after Carey had died, Charles Haddon Spurgeon was born in a thatched cottage in the small village of Kelvedon in Essex. In many ways these two giants of Baptist history are very different: Carey, the humble shoemaker turned missionary pioneer; Spurgeon, the renowned pastor and prince of preachers. Carey was shy and retiring; Spurgeon was a volcano of a personality, bursting with energy.

Yet both men drank deeply from the wells of divine grace. Both were committed unflinchingly to the sovereignty of God, but neither could abide the lifeless traditionalism that stifled the cause of evangelism. Both were men of compassion and love. They proclaimed a holistic gospel addressed to living persons, soul and body, in all of their broken humanity and need for wholeness. In their own day, and since then, their influence and witness have extended far beyond the bounds of the Baptist family. Though they are long dead, like Abel they still speak (Heb. 11:4). Their lives still glitter with grace.

Carey's mission to India inspired many others to carry the good news of Christ into all the world—David Livingstone in Africa, Henry Martyn in Persia, Lottie Moon and Hudson Taylor in China. But the movement for world evangelization also provoked a revival of the very attitude Carey had confronted as a young pastor in England. Matthew 28:19–20 again became a battleground. Some saw it as an obscure text with little relevance for the contemporary church. Others found in it the marching orders for every Christian. Spurgeon belonged enthusiastically to the latter group. He spoke strongly against those who ignored and abused the clear meaning of Jesus' words:

> I have met with some brethren who have tried to read the Bible the wrong way upwards. They have said, "God has a purpose which is certain to be fulfilled, therefore we will not budge an inch. All power is in the hands of Christ, therefore we will sit still"; but that is not Christ's way of reading the passage. It is, "All power is given unto me, *therefore go ye*, and do something."[14]

> The lazy-bones of our orthodox churches cry, "God will do his own work"; and then they look out the softest pillow they can find, and put it under their heads, and say, "The eternal purposes will be carried out: God will be glorified." That is all very fine talk, but it can be used with the most mischievous design. You can make opium out of it, which will

lull you into a deep and dreadful slumber and prevent your being of any kind of use at all.[15]

Spurgeon was a megachurch pastor before megachurches were cool. In his forty years of ministry, he preached to some ten million people. Each week thousands crowded into the Metropolitan Tabernacle in London to listen to his sermons. On Sunday nights the crowds grew so large that Spurgeon had to ask his own members to stay at home, or to gather for prayer in other places, so that the throngs of visitors could find a seat! Spurgeon appealed to them all—from paupers and street urchins to statesmen and peers of the realm. On one occasion, Queen Victoria herself put on a disguise and came to the Tabernacle.

Spurgeon was unique, and it would be foolish for any pastor to try to imitate his style today. But we do need a revival of the kind of God-intoxicated, grace-filled preaching that marked Spurgeon's ministry. What was Spurgeon's preaching like? It was biblical, Trinitarian, promiscuous, urgent, and compassionate.

Biblical

Spurgeon lived in a day when arguing about the Bible and theology was much in vogue. He was aware of these currents of thought, but they seldom showed up in his preaching. He knew that it was futile to try to prove God by an intellectual demonstration. Spurgeon knew that God had revealed his will in Holy Scripture, and that preaching had to be an exposition of the Bible. The preacher must speak *from* the Bible, and not just *about* it. His job is not to give a learned discourse on history, apologetics, ethics, current events, or anything else, but rather to declare an unequivocal "Thus saith the Lord." I like the story of the little eight-year-old boy who was taken to hear Spurgeon preach. His father told him that he was about to hear the greatest preacher in the world. When it was over, the boy said, "I know how to be the greatest preacher in the world." "How?" asked his father. "Why, just pick out a nice chapter in the Bible, and tell just what is in it so that everybody can understand you, and nothing more."[16]

Trinitarian

Because Spurgeon's preaching was so thoroughly biblical, it was also inherently Trinitarian. He never ceased to magnify the one God who is Father, Son, and Holy Spirit, the God of creation, redemption, and consummation. Spurgeon knew, of course, that the heart of the gospel is Jesus Christ, and he never tired of lifting him up. He once said, "A Christless gospel is no gospel and a Christless discourse is the cause of merriment to devils. . . . Jesus, Jesus, Jesus, only have we laboured to extol."[17] But what Jesus did Spurgeon preach? If Jesus were not the divine Son of God, co-eternal with the Father and the Holy Spirit, his work on the cross would have had no more salvific value than the death of Socrates. Spurgeon frequently began his sermons with this prayer, which shows the deep Trinitarian structure of his whole understanding of the Christian life:

> To the one God of heaven and earth in the Trinity of his sacred Persons be all honor and glory world without end; to the Glorious Father, as the Covenant God of Israel; to the Gracious Son, the Redeemer of his people; to the Holy Ghost, the Author of Sanctification, be everlasting praise for that gospel of free grace proclaimed unto all through Jesus Christ our Lord. Amen.

We can get out of biblical balance by overemphasizing one of the divine persons to the exclusion of the other two. Classical Unitarianism proclaims "the Fatherhood of God and the brotherhood of man" but reduces Jesus to a pious teacher and the Holy Spirit to an impersonal idea. Some "Jesus only" denominations collapse the Trinity into Christ, while certain Pentecostal and charismatic churches so exalt the Spirit that the Father and the Son are ignored. Spurgeon knew that the gospel of free grace requires us to pay equal attention to all three members of the Holy Trinity in the unity of their redeeming work.

Promiscuous

The word *promiscuous* has a very negative meaning as we most often use it today. It refers to someone who is unrestrained in sexual immorality, one who carries on illicit affairs with many persons. But the word itself means simply "having different elements mixed or mingled together, indiscriminate." In this sense, Spurgeon's preaching was promiscuous in its scope. He believed that the good news of the gospel was intended to be proclaimed indiscriminately to all persons everywhere.

As we have seen, this flew in the face of the hyper-Calvinistic practice of addressing the claims of the gospel to the elect only. Spurgeon pointed out that in the Bible the gospel was preached to human beings not as elect or non-elect, but simply as sinners in need of redemption. In his sermon on Mars Hill, Paul was emphatic that God "commands all people everywhere to repent." And he linked this universal call for repentance with the future judgment God has appointed for the whole world (see Acts 17:30–31). Like Carey before him, Spurgeon believed that the Great Commission is universal in its outreach. We are to preach the gospel to every creature, not merely to those already regenerated or to those we suppose may be in the number of the elect. Such speculation is both foolish and dangerous.

One of Spurgeon's favorite Bible verses was John 6:37: "Him that cometh to me I will in no wise cast out" (KJV). Like Carey's "Expect great things, attempt great things" watchword, this verse holds divine sovereignty and human responsibility together in beautiful equipoise. Spurgeon preached many sermons from this text. Here is a sample from one of them:

Sinners, let me address you with words of life; Jesus wants nothing from you, nothing whatsoever, nothing done, nothing felt; he gives both work and feeling. Ragged, penniless, just as you are, lost, forsaken, desolate, with no good feelings, and no good hopes, Jesus still comes to you, and in these words of pity he addresses you, "Him that cometh unto me I will in no wise cast out." . . . "Him that cometh to me" . . . the man may have been guilty of an atrocious sin, but if he comes to Christ he shall not be cast out. I cannot tell what kind of persons may have come into this hall tonight; but if burglars, murderers, and dynamite-men were here, I would still bid them come to Christ, for he will not cast them out. No limit is set to the extent of sin: Any "him" in all the world—any blaspheming, devilish "him" that comes to Christ shall be welcomed. I use strong words that I may open the gate of mercy. Any "him" that comes to Christ—though he come from slum or taproom, betting-ring or gambling-hall, prison or brothel—Jesus will in no wise cast out.[18]

Urgent

For Spurgeon a sermon was not a lecture but a summons, divinely sent, with eternal consequences in the balance. This is why he preached with an urgency and passion that was riveting to his hearers. In Spurgeon's day, there were those who felt the preacher's task was done once he had presented the bare facts of the gospel. Spurgeon knew that this way of thinking did not mesh with the pattern of apostolic preaching in the Bible. Why did Paul say, "The love of Christ compels us" (2 Cor. 5:14, NIV)? Why did he consider his life worth nothing? Why did he weep night and day as he presented the gospel to the people of Ephesus (see Acts 20:31)? The true presentation of the gospel must be more than the dispensing of information. It must be an invitation. This invitation is not like inviting someone to go to a concert or to go bowling. This invitation comes not from the preacher, but from God. This invitation cannot be equated with walking the aisle or shaking the pastor's hand, though God can and does use such public expressions to draw lost sinners unto himself. This invitation is extended by Jesus himself. It comes from the Scriptures through the preacher. It is extended by the Holy Spirit, who convicts the sinner and draws him or her to the fountain of grace.

Compassionate

The Dutch theologian Herman Bavinck wrote that the gospel is "so powerful that it cannot be conquered, so loving it excludes all force."[19] This is also an apt description of Spurgeon's preaching. It was filled with compassion, tenderheartedness, and a constant appeal to the love of God. Those who restrict the love of God only to the elect are impugning an essential element of his divine character. Only three times in the Bible is God directly equated with some particular reality other than one of his personal names: God is light, God is a consuming fire, and God is love (1 John 1:5; Heb. 12:29; 1 John 4:16).

Spurgeon's heart was ablaze with the love of God, and this was evident in his love for the lost.

> "We win by love," Spurgeon said. "We win hearts for Jesus by love, by sympathy with their sorrows, by anxiety lest they should perish, by pleading with God for them with all our hearts that they would not be left to die unsaved, by pleading with God for them that, for their own sake, they would seek mercy and find grace."[20]

These were not merely words from the pulpit. They reflected a lifestyle of compassion and neighborly love that took with utmost seriousness every person created in the image of God. Long before the term *social ministry* was in vogue, Spurgeon was reaching out with the love of Jesus to orphans and unwanted children, to women of the gutter, to the nameless nobodies who crowded the streets of Victorian London. The demands of his ministry were staggering, but he was never too busy to counsel with the troubled soul, to pray with the sick, to visit the bereaved.

Such acts of mercy gave authenticity to his preaching about grace. No one has ever accused Spurgeon of ignoring theology or being soft on doctrine. But he was wise enough to know that doctrine alone is not enough. "When love dies," he said, "orthodox doctrine becomes a corpse, a powerless formalism. Adhesion to the truth sours into bigotry when the sweetness and light of love to Jesus depart. . . . Lose love, lose all."[21]

LEARNING FROM THE PAST

It is now well over one hundred years since Spurgeon died, and more than two hundred years since Carey's mission to India. Today the Christian world stands again at a critical juncture in the fulfillment of the Great Commission. At Beeson Divinity School, there is a digital world population clock, which electronically ticks out the number of people on earth second by second, number by number. It is a chilling experience to stand in front of that clock and see the rapidly changing numbers, each one representing a soul that will spend eternity either with God or separated from him. Of the nearly seven billion persons on earth, as many as one-third of them have never heard the name of Jesus.

Carey burned with compassion for the lost world, for those who were perishing without Christ. He knew that the grace of God was not the private possession of the frozen chosen, the cozy elect. It was good news, the best news possible, amazing news of a gracious God who loved so deeply that in his absolute freedom and sovereignty he chose to show mercy rather than execute justice (which he may well have done by right) against guilty sinners. Carey went to India to proclaim by word and deed this glorious gospel—the good news of a God who brings sinners from unimaginable misery into unimaginable glory *sola gratia*, "by grace alone"! Today, more than anything else, the church of Jesus Christ needs a fresh vision of Carey's God—a full-sized God, eternal, transcendent, holy, filled with compassion, sovereignly working by his Holy Spirit to call unto himself a people out of every nation, kindred, tribe, and language group on earth. Only such a vision, born of repentance, prayer, and self-denial, can inspire a Carey-like faith in this new generation.

As Spurgeon grew older, his battle for gospel preaching intensified. He became embroiled in a major theological dispute known as the Down Grade Controversy. This was brought about by the unwarranted concessions some Christian leaders were making to the rising tide of liberal theology. Fundamental issues of the historic Christian faith were under attack from those who no longer found them "relevant" to the needs of the church. The person and work of Christ were denigrated, and the total truthfulness of Scripture was denied. Jesus' substitutionary atonement was relegated to the dustbin of theory. Spurgeon resisted this doctrinal laxity and error. He endeavored to stave off "the boiling mudshowers of modern heresy," which were beginning to descend on church life in his day.[22] In hyper-Calvinism Spurgeon had encountered a rationalism of the right, a theology so enthralled with the power of God that it lost sight of his love. Now, in the Down Grade Controversy, he came face-to-face with a rationalism of the left, an antisupernaturalist ideology that eviscerated the heart of the gospel itself.

Confronted with this new challenge, Spurgeon looked back on some of the earlier disputes between Calvinists and Arminians and he saw them in a different light. "We used to debate on particular and general redemption," he said, "but now men question whether there is any redemption at all worthy of the name."[23] To the end of his life, Spurgeon continued to preach both the sovereignty of God in salvation and the universal love of God for the lost. God did not create human beings to be damned. If they are damned (and Spurgeon believed in an actual, eternal hell), their damnation is all of them. But if they are saved, their salvation is all of God. Some people accused Spurgeon of being a rigid Calvinist because he did believe and preach the doctrines of grace. Others called him an Arminian because he stressed human responsibility and preached the gospel indiscriminately to all.

Was Spurgeon really inconsistent? No more or less so than the Bible itself. The theology of grace in Christian history oscillates between the poles of divine sovereignty and human responsibility. Both are biblical and evangelical truths that must be held in tension if the gospel is to be proclaimed in its purity and urgency. Spurgeon was willing to live with that tension, knowing that one day in heaven, if we need to know how this deep mystery is resolved in God's own mind, he will reveal it to us in his own time and in his own way. In one of his last sermons at the Metropolitan Tabernacle, Spurgeon looked back over the years of his ministry and remarked:

> I have endeavored, in my ministry, to preach to you, not a part of the truth, but the whole counsel of God; but I cannot harmonize it, nor am I anxious to do so. I am sure all truth is harmonious, and *to my ear* the harmony is clear enough; but I cannot give you a complete score of the music, or mark the harmonies on the gamut. I must leave the Chief Musician to do that.[24]

{ *Six* }

LIVING BY GRACE

*I feel that, if I could live a thousand lives, I would like to live
them all for Christ, and I should even then feel that they were
all too little a return for his great love to me.*[1]
~ CHARLES HADDON SPURGEON

God's grace is always purposeful, never capricious or haphazard. God has a purpose for all believers who have been saved by grace. What is that purpose? It is this: that they should "be conformed to the image of his Son" (Rom. 8:29). J. B. Phillips renders that verse in this way: "God, in his foreknowledge, chose them to bear the family likeness of his Son, that he might be the eldest of a family of many brothers." This means that grace is operative in the life of the believer not only at the moment of conversion but all the way through our Christian experience. Not only are we saved by grace, but we are meant to live by grace too. This is why the Bible says that we are to "grow in the grace and knowledge of our Lord and Savior Jesus Christ" (2 Pet. 3:18).

Paul has this same thought in mind when writing to the Christians in Galatia. In a startling image, he compares his ministry among them to a mother undergoing the pains of childbirth "until Christ is formed in you" (Gal. 4:19). The Greek word translated "formed" is *morphoō*, a medical term for the growth of a fetus into an infant. Paul is deeply concerned about these new believers. He does not want them to suffer a spiritual miscarriage but desires instead that they make their calling and election sure. Paul assumes that they have indeed been born again, that Christ is in them already. But Christ must continue to be formed in them just as they are being formed in him. They need to grow in grace, in Christlikeness. They need to experience more and more "the life of God in the soul of man," as the title of Henry Scougal's classic book on spirituality puts it. The great evangelist George Whitefield understood this when he wrote in his journal, "God soon showed me . . . that 'true religion was union of the soul with God, and Christ formed within us.' "[2]

In this concluding chapter, we are going to look at several questions that have arisen throughout this study on what it means to live by grace. Before we begin this review, however, let's look briefly at some of the ground we have covered already.

In chapter 1 we began our study by defining *grace* as God's free and sovereign favor to ill-deserving sinners. We also saw how grace is consonant with the character of God himself and how it fills every aspect of his long-range plan of salvation. In chapter 2 we took up the theme of divine providence. We saw how God governs the course of history both by direct intervention and through the freely chosen acts of human beings created in his image. We also saw how God uses suffering and tragedy as occasions to display his glory. This principle is evident throughout the Bible, but nowhere more clearly than in the event of Jesus' crucifixion, where God used the most horrible event imaginable, the brutalizing death of his own Son, to fulfill his perfect plan of redemption.

Next, in chapter 3, we looked at some of the debates Christians have carried on among themselves about the nature of grace and how it works in relation to human freedom. We found Augustine's thoughts very helpful on this subject, though we could not follow his theology in every detail. We also considered how Christians who hold differing views on the details of predestination may nonetheless stand united in Christ and work together in sharing the gospel with the lost. In chapter 4 we reviewed some of the ways the doctrines of grace have been seen historically, and we looked briefly at two serious deviations from the biblical doctrine of grace—legalism and antinomianism.

In chapter 5, we looked at the meaning of grace in relation to the Great Commission. We pointed out how those who use God's grace as an excuse for laziness and inaction are really perverters of the good news itself. We saw how William Carey overcame obstinate opposition to carry the gospel into all the world. And we also looked at Charles Haddon Spurgeon, the prince of preachers, who proclaimed God's illimitable love to "whosoever will" while never denying God's sovereign grace in the salvation of every sinner who comes to Christ. Let's look now at some of the questions that have arisen in our study.

WHAT'S SO AMAZING ABOUT GRACE?

This question is the title of a book published by Philip Yancey several years ago. It suggests that for many people there is really nothing about grace sufficiently amazing to justify that adjective. Sadly, this is true for thousands of folks, including many who have grown up around the church. They have grown up with the language of grace and the music of grace, but their hearts have grown hardened to the true reality of grace. They suffer from grace inflation. God's love and mercy no longer amaze, astound, and shatter. They have become deaf to its melodies and blind to its glories. For people like this, it may take a tragedy or an emergency to shatter the myth of self-sufficiency with which they have "protected" themselves from the wooings of grace. When people are flat on their backs, they can only look up. In such a moment, their need for God may be revealed, and they will see, perhaps for the first time, three amazing facts about grace.

It's Undeserved!

In our modern industrialized societies, almost everything is based on what might be called "a theology of grabs." If you want to get ahead in business, then you must claw your way up the organization. If you want to succeed in politics, you'd better grab the initiative from your opponent, destroying him in the process if possible. Feminism says to women, "Grab the power from the men." Even children are told that they may sue their parents and grab authority for themselves. Many people carry this same "theology of grabs" into the spiritual realm, assuming that they can relate to God on a quid pro quo basis. But the Bible tells another story. It says that God is too great and holy, and that our sins are too deep and dark, to allow this kind of bargaining at the barricade of salvation.

Jesus told a parable about a man who owned a vineyard (see Matt. 20:1–16). The man went out early one morning and hired some laborers to work in his field. Around noontime he brought on a second shift; then again, right before closing, he hired a few more stragglers and put them to work. At the end of the day, everyone was paid the same amount! Those who had toiled all day in the sun were furious. "We deserve much more than these Johnny-come-latelies!" they exclaimed. They were amazed, and quite upset, at the generosity of the owner toward these ill-deserving workers. The disgruntled workers' argument makes perfect sense in "the kingdom of grabs." But not in the kingdom of grace. Here we learn that God does not play by our rules. The vineyard is his. The fact that he calls us at all is a matter of sheer grace, his undeserved favor. If God blesses us with good things, including salvation, it is not because of the hours worked, the effort expended, or the merits earned. It is all grace, grace undeserved, as

Augustus Toplady expressed it in his classic hymn, "Rock of Ages, Cleft for Me":

> Not the labors of my hands
> Can fulfil Thy law's demands;
> Could my zeal no respite know,
> Could my tears forever flow,
> All for sin could not atone;
> Thou must save, and Thou alone.[3]

It's Unexpected!

The grouchy workers in Jesus' parable expected one thing and got something else. In Ezekiel 37, God shows the prophet a valley of dry bones, the desiccated remnants of a once-great army. "Can these bones live?" the Lord asks Ezekiel. The prophet replies, "O Lord GOD, you know." At God's command, Ezekiel speaks his word. The Spirit blows across the valley. The unexpected, the impossible, happens: the army comes to life again!

The story of Racehoss Sample illustrates how God's grace works unexpectedly in human lives. Racehoss was the son of Big Emma, a Texas prostitute who beat and abused her unwanted child until he ran away from home at age eleven. He lived like a bum until he joined the army. Soon he went AWOL and was eventually sentenced to thirty years in the Texas State Penitentiary for assault and battery. He was so rough that he had to be placed in solitary confinement, a filthy pit of absolute darkness. In this hellhole, he was reduced to the level of an animal groveling for the morsels of food thrown down to him from time to time. In the midst of desperation, he cried one day, "Help me, God! Help meeeee!" Here is how he described what happened next:

> A ray of light between my fingers. Slowly uncovering my face, the whole cell was illuminated like a 40-watt bulb turned on. The soft light soothed

me and I no longer was afraid. Engulfed by a presence, I felt it reassuring me. It comforted me . . . I breathed freely. I had never felt such well-being, so good, in all my life. Safe. Loved.

The voice within talked through the pit of my belly. "You are not an animal. You are a human being." And "Don't you worry about a thing. But you must tell them about me."

After that, God was real. He found me in the abyss of the burning hell, uplifted and fed my hungry soul, and breathed new life into my nostrils.[4]

On January 12, 1972, Racehoss walked out of prison a free man and a new creation in Christ. He later served as a probation officer and was named the Outstanding Crime Prevention Citizen of Texas in 1981. Later he received a full pardon. The story of Racehoss Sample is unique. His conversion to Christ was unusual and dramatic. But it reminds us that God's grace can break through the most impenetrable barriers in the most unexpected manner.

It's Inexplicable!

Several times in this study we have encountered the word *mystery*. A mystery is something we know to be true because God has revealed it to be so in his Word, but we cannot explain it or account for it in terms of our human rationality and logic. God's grace is inexplicable in this way. This is why Paul's theology turns into doxology at the end of Romans 11. After dealing extensively with the profound issues of predestination and grace, he throws up his hands, as it were, and exclaims:

Frankly, I stand amazed at the unfathomable complexity of God's wisdom and God's knowledge. How could man ever understand his reasons for action, or explain his methods of working? . . . For of him, and through

him, and unto him, are all things. To him be the glory forever, amen.
(Rom. 11:33, 36, PHILLIPS)

WHY TALK ABOUT PREDESTINATION?

If we will never be able to fully explain the mystery of divine grace this side of heaven, then why should we talk about such thorny issues as predestination, God's eternal decrees, and the like? There are two answers to this question. It is right to study these doctrines because they are biblically significant and pastorally relevant.

Several years ago I visited Thomas Jefferson's famous home at Monticello. While going through his library, we were shown a copy of Jefferson's New Testament. Jefferson had gone through with a pen and marked out all the references that offended him, all the verses about God's wrath, hell, judgment, and so forth. While no Bible-believing Christian would be so impudent as Jefferson in actually deleting a part of God's Word, in reality we are guilty of a similar offense when we deliberately ignore any portion of what God has revealed to us in Scripture. We are not free to ignore the doctrine of predestination simply because we do not like it, cannot understand it, or do not see how it can be squared with a particular philosophical understanding of reality. If we affirm the verbal inspiration of the Bible, as we should, then we know that God has wasted no words in revealing his will to us. There are many doctrinal truths we may not be able to understand perfectly in this life, but God has revealed them to us for a purpose. It is our duty to rightly divide the Word of truth so that we may understand it more fully and thus love and serve God more faithfully until in heaven we shall see "face to face" (1 Cor. 13:12).

The doctrine of grace is not only biblically significant; it's also pastorally relevant. Paul discovered that God's grace was sufficient in the extremities of his life, and so it has been for Christians through the ages. Some years ago a good friend stopped by my office to share with me the shattering news he had just received: his wife was leaving him and his children for another man. I didn't know how to respond or what to say. But I remember mumbling, "I love you, and there is grace." More recently, one of my colleagues came to see me after a serious bout with cancer. He said to me: "Timothy, I have preached about grace all my life, but now I know its meaning more deeply than I ever have before. I have been to the bottom, and I can tell you that it is solid." Both of these friends learned through experience the powerful promise God made to Israel long ago:

> Fear not, for I have redeemed you;
>> I have called you by name, you are mine.
> When you pass through the waters, I will be with you; . . .
> when you walk through fire you shall not be burned,
>> and the flame shall not consume you. (Isa. 43:1–2)

WHY SHOULD WE PRAY?

All Christians pray. We begin our walk with God by crying out, "Lord, be merciful to me a sinner." We grow step-by-step in our relationship with God as our hearts become centered on him. We hear him speak to us by his Spirit through the Scriptures, and we respond in petition, intercession, confession, and praise. We know that God wants us to pray and that he hears and responds to us when we do pray. A Christian who does not pray is like a bird that cannot fly or a fire that does not burn.

T. W. Hunt has said that "prayer must be built on the foundation of the sovereignty and character of God."[5] We have no "right" to approach God on our own, apart from Christ, for our sins have placed an unbridgeable gulf between him and us. We dare to come to the throne of grace only because we are invited to do so by the God who is limitless in his love, as well as awesome in his holiness. Still, though, the question persists: If God is truly omniscient, knowing everything that will happen before it occurs, why should we pray?

What difference do our prayers make? Wouldn't everything turn out just the same if we never prayed at all? Doesn't God's initiative in loving, choosing, redeeming, calling, and preserving his children invalidate their need to respond to him in prayer?

These questions have been asked through the ages, and they deserve a straightforward response. That response is simple: God foreknows and chooses the means as well as the end, and our prayers are one of the foreordained means he has chosen to bring to pass what he has sovereignly intended. Again, we may not be able to explain perfectly how our prayers and God's purpose work together compatibly to accomplish what God of his own "good pleasure" has determined, but that this is so we can have no doubt, for it is clearly attested in Scripture (Luke 12:32).

Second Corinthians 1:8–11 is one of many passages where this principle is clearly set forth. In these verses, Paul tells the believers in Corinth about terrible hardships and sufferings he has recently endured in his missionary travels. Some of these were so severe that he did not think he would survive. But he can see God's purpose and plan behind it all: "But this happened that we might not rely on ourselves but on God, who raises the dead" (v. 9, NIV). In the meantime, the Lord has delivered him from this peril and will, he believes, continue to sustain him and enable him to proclaim the gospel to others. But how will God do this? Paul's answer is clear: "He will continue to deliver us, *as you help us by your prayers*. Then many will give thanks on our behalf for the gracious favor granted us in answer to the prayers of many" (vv. 10–11, NIV). The Corinthian Christians were praying for Paul, and God used their prayers to rescue him from imminent danger.

When we pray for missionaries we have never seen, some of whom are serving Christ in faraway places, we should remember that God uses our prayers to strengthen and encourage his servants and to remove obstacles to the progress of the gospel that human willpower alone could never budge.

Does God still work through the prayers of his people to accomplish the spread of the gospel around the world? Several years ago Sheila King Everett and her pastor-husband Randel were serving the First Baptist Church of Benton, Arkansas. A young woman in Sheila's Sunday school class who was preparing to go to Europe as a missionary with Campus Crusade for Christ requested prayer for the country of Albania. At that time Albania was totally atheistic and closed to all Christian influences. "From that time on," Sheila said, "God put it on my heart to start praying. I started praying that God would break down the walls of Albania."[6]

Not long after that, the International Mission Board of the Southern Baptist Convention began asking churches to "adopt" unreached people groups around the world. They were asked to pray that God would make a way for the gospel to be taken to a specific group or nation. One Wednesday night, Randel announced to the congregation that they had been assigned to pray for the people of Albania. "I almost shouted," Sheila said. "Some would say this was just a random assignment, but I wouldn't."[7] Not long after this, the Everetts were called to serve a church in Fort Worth, Texas, and there they met David and Mary Carpenter, a young professional couple who had sold their home and left their comfortable lifestyle to prepare for what they believed was a definite call from God to share his love with the people of Albania. When they compared notes with the Everetts, the Carpenters realized that the timing of their sense of God's call on their lives was not random. It coincided with Sheila's burden to pray for Albania.

In September 1992 the Carpenters finally made it to Albania. They were among the first Christian missionaries to enter that formerly closed country. Today there are hundreds of Christian missionaries bearing witness to the gospel in that land, where the dogma of atheism once reigned supreme. In the capital city of Tirana, the radio tower that used to broadcast the propaganda of the Communist Party now emits a different signal as the life-giving gospel of grace sounds forth. Looking back on all this, Sheila sees a confirmation of the way prayer can make a difference in the life of an individual and in the course of a nation. "I definitely believe God uses prayer to open up the hearts of people, to open up countries that haven't been opened or ethnic groups that haven't been opened. It's made me believe in his sovereignty even that much more."[8]

DOES GRACE HAVE ANYTHING TO DO WITH WORSHIP?

During the past decades the evangelical church has been beset by a raucous controversy over the nature of public worship. Should we use praise choruses or sing only standard hymns in church? Should we use drums and guitars or only the piano and organ? Is it okay to lift your hands in worship? What about kneeling for prayer? Do we process with banners, or not process at all? Questions like these have led to "worship wars" in many places, and quite a few congregations have been torn asunder trying to deal with them. A true appreciation of the grace of God will help us to see these matters in the right perspective. Grace helps us to refocus on the main issue, which is not style of music, order of worship, or some other external factor, but rather our motivation for worship and the nature of the God we dare to approach.

The prophet Malachi wrote his prophecy in response to a crisis of worship among the children of Israel. He begins by announcing a burdensome message from the Lord ("burden" is a better translation than "oracle" for the Hebrew word *masa'* in Mal. 1:1). It is the burden of love. "I have loved you," says the Lord. Here we have a solemn declaration of the sovereign Lord. He has loved and chosen Israel to be his people despite their many wanderings, backslidings, and sins. God's love is unconditional. He does not love them because of anything they have done for him. He loves them freely, completely, undeservedly. This is grace!

The children of Israel make a twofold response to the love God has lavished upon them. First of all, they question it. "But you say, 'How have you loved us?'" (Mal. 1:2). In other words, they say to the Lord, "You don't really love us, do you God?" They question God's love because it is too radical and free. Their God is a contract God of wages and labor, not the covenant God of mercy and grace. Like the unhappy workers in Jesus' parable, they have made a bargain with God. They will do this if he will do that. They want to squeeze every ounce possible out of this deal they have made with the deity. This is the attitude they bring to worship and it leads to exhaustion and compromise. Second, when they come to God's house, they bring "defiled food" to place on his altar—crippled lambs, blind and diseased animals, the leftovers of their flock. God will not accept such offerings, and he tells them it would be better to close the doors of the temple completely than to carry on such a charade in his house (see Mal. 1:10). In the midst of the crisis, someone says, "And now entreat the favor of God, that he may be gracious to us" (Mal. 1:9). They have forgotten that God *was* gracious to them. They would never have returned from exile apart from God's grace. They would have no temple at all without God's favor and love. God did not need any of their sacrifices for he owns the cattle on a thousand hills. But the God of grace who needs nothing wants everything—their hearts, their lives, their love. This is why he would not accept their puny animals and stingy sacrifices.

Once we understand who God really is, once we have experienced his inexhaustible lovingkindness, which, like the dew, is fresh every morning, it will change the way we worship. From a heart overflowing with gratitude, we will want to honor and glorify God by gratefully offering back to him the many good gifts he has bestowed on us. We will not go to church to be entertained, to see "what we can get out of it" for our own private gratification, but rather to praise and worship the triune God of grace and glory.

Several years ago I taught a course on worship for students preparing to be pastors and worship leaders. I asked them to visit two congregations of contrasting worship styles and to bring back a report to the class on each one. I shall never forget what one of the students reported. His first case study was a wealthy suburban congregation, well heeled in every way. He was welcomed avidly as a new prospect, but he felt a kind of smugness in the worship. The church had many activities and was doing many wonderful things, but the service seemed more focused on the worshipers themselves than on God. This even showed up in the morning prayer as the pastor reminded God of how busy the congregation had been in their service for him—the building program, mission trips, the youth retreat in the Rockies, and so forth. When it was over, the student said he felt as if he had been to a pep rally or a motivational meeting.

His next assignment was a tiny African American congregation in the inner city. The building was dilapidated and the pews uncomfortable. Here too he was warmly welcomed, but he noticed a different tone in the worship. This congregation had obviously experienced a great deal of hardship and struggle, but there was a sense of joy in their singing and a note of absolute dependence on God in their prayers. This was evident in the traditional prayer-chant that began the morning service. As the whole church moaned in prayer, an elderly deacon said:

Oh Lord, I thank you that when I woke up this morning, my bed was not my cooling board, nor my blanket my winding sheet. I just want to praise you and glorify you because the blood was flowing warm through my veins. Lord, you've been so good to us. We've had enough coal to keep us warm this winter. We've had enough food to keep us from starving to death. You're an awesome God! And Lord, we're just

so glad to be here this morning! We're so thankful that you let us come
to this service one more time!

No one should misunderstand this real-life illustration. True
worship is not a matter of rich versus poor, white versus black, or
inner city versus suburban. No doubt there are inner-city churches
whose worship is choked with pride and self-sufficiency, just as there
are suburban churches alive with the reality of God's presence. But
our sense of the grace of God, of our neediness in the face of his
omnipotent love, is a true barometer of genuine spirituality and biblical worship.

WHAT ARE THE MARKS OF A GRACIOUS CHRISTIAN?

Two of the best books on living by grace are Chuck Swindoll's *Grace
Awakening* and Jerry Bridges's *Transforming Grace*. Both titles point
to the fact that God's grace is an active, life-changing reality. In its
deepest meaning, this is what the word *gracious* connotes—not just
courteous or polite, but filled with compassion, radiating kindness,
winsome in all ways. This quality cannot be learned by going to a
charm school or by reading a "how-to" manual. No, it is the fruit of
the Holy Spirit. It comes about when a person is so thoroughly grasped
by grace that he or she becomes a channel through which God's great
love shines forth in relationships with others. The more we see our
own unworthiness, the more astounded we are at God's gracious favor
and mercy toward us. And the more we realize that our life-purpose
must be to glorify God, to please him in every way, the more others
will notice the results of God's transforming grace in our lives. They
will see us shaped, more and more, by these five marks:

1. A grateful heart. The word *gratitude* comes from the Latin root
gratus, which means "pleasing" or "thankful." It is closely related to

the Latin word for grace, *gratia*. One of the surest marks of a soul touched by grace is the desire to say "thank you" to God. When Jesus healed ten men of leprosy, only one of them came back to thank him. Jesus asked, "Where are the nine?" (Luke 17:11–19). The other nine had been cleansed outwardly but their hearts remained tough and unchanged. We express our gratitude to God with our lives as well as our lips. The opposite of gratitude is jealousy. It stems from our thinking that somehow God has given someone else what should rightly be ours. But this is to disparage what God has given us, to consider it worthless, of no value compared with what we think we should have had. There is no place for jealousy in the family of God for we have nothing that we did not receive. Our heavenly Father makes no mistakes in dispensing good gifts to his children.

2. A humble countenance. My wife and I once entertained a visiting preacher in our home. He kept on saying, "I'm just a humble pastor, you know." Soon we realized that this man was bragging about his humility! But true humility is more elusive than that. Once you capture it and begin to admire it, you've already lost it. Genuine humility is a by-product of our walk with God. It is a quality others recognize in us when we ourselves may not even be aware of it. The opposite of humility is puffed-up arrogance, which results from thinking more highly of ourselves than we should. As we have seen throughout this study, even the theology of grace can become an occasion for self-congratulations and pride. I have encountered this attitude on both sides of the Calvinist-Arminian divide. John Wesley and Charles Haddon Spurgeon were on opposite sides of this debate, but they both urged their followers to season their zeal for doctrinal purity with a good dose of humility. Wesley said to his disciples, "Is it not the duty of every Arminian Preacher . . . never, in public or in private, to use the word *Calvinist* as a term of reproach; seeing it is neither better nor worse than calling names?—a practice no more consistent with good sense or good manners, than it is with Christianity."[9] For his part, Spurgeon recognized that many Arminians were godly Christians while some Calvinists were "as proud as Lucifer." "Far be it from me," Spurgeon said, "even to imagine that Zion contains none but Calvinistic Christians within her walls, or that there are none saved who do not hold our views."[10]

3. A forgiving spirit. The glorious message of the gospel is that the almighty God of heaven has bound himself to lost sinners in a relationship of the freest and most perfect grace. At the heart of this relationship is forgiveness, as the psalmist knew long ago:

> Blessed is the one whose transgression is forgiven,
>> whose sin is covered.
> Blessed is the man against whom the LORD counts no iniquity.
>> (Ps. 32:1–2)

Receiving God's forgiveness has a catalytic effect in our relationships with others. Paul makes this clear in Ephesians 4:32: "Be kind to one another, tenderhearted, forgiving one another, as God in Christ forgave you." To harbor grudges against other people, to seek revenge, and to bear resentment and bitterness for wrongs suffered in the past are telltale signs that one is not living by grace. The elder brother would not go into the party and rejoice at the return of his wayward sibling, and so he remained estranged from his father's love. How we relate horizontally to our brothers and sisters here on earth says a great deal about our vertical relationship with our Father in heaven (see 1 John 3:11–15).

4. A life of love. Over one hundred years ago Henry Drummond, the Scottish evangelist and friend of D. L. Moody, published a devotional exposition of 1 Corinthians 13. He called it *The Greatest Thing in the World.* That little book has never been out of print. It still speaks powerfully of the importance of love in the Christian life. Drummond rightly recognized that the kind of love Paul describes in I Corinthians 13 is not a mere human achievement but rather a graciously given divine gift. It is not something we have the capacity to produce on our own, but only the capacity to receive by God's grace. Even so, Drummond said, Christian love is an effect, the cause of which is God's extraordinary love for us.

> "We love—because He first loved us." Look at that word "because." . . . "*Because* He first loved us," the effect follows that we love, we love Him, we love all men. We cannot help it. Because He loved us, we love, we love everybody. Our heart is slowly changed. Contemplate the love of Christ, and you will love. Stand before that mirror, reflect Christ's character, and you will be changed into the same image from tenderness to tenderness. There is no other way. You cannot love to order. You can only look at the lovely object, and fall in love with it, and grow into likeness to it.[11]

A life of love will reflect a proper balance between grace and truth. Some Christians are big on grace but soft on truth. They glide over the Bible's warnings about the wrath of God and the future judgment that awaits those who reject Christ. On the other hand, there are some other Christians who are great champions of truth, but they have little to say about grace. They are straitlaced in doctrine all right, but they wear their convictions like a straitjacket! They have not learned how to relax into grace. Nor have they learned the wisdom of Francis Schaeffer, who reminded us that "we must not forget that the final end is not what we are against, but what we are for."[12] A gracious life marked by love has ample room for both grace and truth. Neither need be sacrificed for the other for they are not enemies, but friends.

5. *A passion for souls*. Throughout this study we have emphasized the congruence and compatibility of God's sovereignty in salvation on the one hand and the responsibility, indeed the duty, of human beings to repent and believe the gospel on the other. No one has said this better than J. C. Ryle, a great Christian leader in nineteenth-century England:

> Everywhere in Scripture it is a leading principle that man can lose his own soul, that if he is lost at last it will be his own fault, and his blood will be on his own head. The same inspired Bible which reveals this doctrine of Election is the Bible which contains the words, "Why will ye die, O house of Israel?"—"Ye will not come unto me, that ye might have life."—"This is the condemnation, that light has come into the world, and men love darkness rather than light, because their deeds were evil" (Ezekiel 18:31; John 5:40; 3:19). The Bible never says that sinners miss heaven because they are not Elect, but because they "neglect the great salvation," and because they will not repent and believe.[13]

Knowing this to be true, every Christian whose life has been changed by the grace of God is called to be a witness of Jesus Christ to the lost. Of course, we cannot save or convert anyone; that is God's business. Nor are we responsible for making up the content of the message out of our own heads. God has clearly revealed the good news of salvation in his infallible Word. The Bible is God's love letter to a lost world. We are in the delivery business. Our job is to make sure that God's love letter is delivered to its intended recipients—and that means every single person in the world. But unlike a regular mailman who has (or should have) no particular interest in the mail he carries, we have a vital interest both in the message we deliver and in the response of those to whom we present it. It was said of the great Puritan pastor Richard Baxter that he preached as a dying man to dying men. A passion for souls is one of the indelible marks of a gracious Christian.

LIVING THE BENEDICTION

It is appropriate that we close this study of the doctrine of grace with a benediction, a word of blessing. And there is none better than what Paul wrote at the conclusion of his second letter to the Corinthian Christians: "The grace of the Lord Jesus Christ and the love of God and the fellowship of the Holy Spirit be with you all" (2 Cor. 13:14). This verse sums up the great drama of redemption from first to last. We focus first on the grace of our Lord Jesus Christ, the divine Son of God who left the security of the Father's bosom in heaven to be born of a virgin girl here on earth. In his life and through his death on the cross, he perfectly fulfilled all the righteous demands of God's law, making atonement through the shedding of his blood. At his resurrection on Easter Sunday, he burst asunder the bonds of death. He ascended back to heaven, where he waits at the Father's side ready to come again in final triumph when the time is right. And what is the source of these mighty acts of grace? Nothing less than the free and radical love of God the Father. And how do we participate in such love? Through the ministry of the Holy Spirit, who convicts and regenerates us, seals and indwells us, fills and empowers us for the journey of faith to which we are called.

When the angels in heaven consider all that this means, they must gasp with wonder. When we who are not merely onlookers but beneficiaries of such amazing grace try to contemplate its full meaning, surely we too are filled with wonder, gratitude, and praise—breathlessly so. Charles Wesley said it best in the last verse of his great hymn, "And Can It Be":

'Tis mystery all! Th'Immortal dies:
Who can explore His strange design?

In vain the firstborn seraph tries
To sound the depths of love divine.
'Tis mercy all! Let earth adore,
Let angel minds inquire no more.[14]

Sola gratia!
Soli Deo gloria!

Notes

Chapter One: Our Gracious God

1. Julia H. Johnston, "Grace Greater than Our Sin," 1910.

2. Ira F. Stanphill, "Room at the Cross for You," ©1946 New Spring, Inc. (ASCAP) (Administered by Brentwood-Benson Music Publishing, Inc.) All rights reserved. Used by permission.

3. John Newton, "Amazing Grace," 1779.

4. Tertullian, "Apology," 39, in *The Ante-Nicene Fathers*, ed. Rev. Alexander Roberts and James Donaldson, vol. 3 (Grand Rapids: Eerdmans, 1980), 46.

5. Arius, quoted in Arthur C. McGill, *Suffering: A Test of Theological Method* (Philadelphia: The Geneva Press, 1968), 64, emphasis added.

6. Martin Luther, quoted in Karl Barth, *Dogmatics in Outline* (New York: Harper and Row, 1959), 54.

7. Thomas Hardy, "The Dynasts," in *The Works of Thomas Hardy in Prose and Verse*, vol. 2 (London: Macmillan, 1913), 254.

8. Oscar Hardman, *The Christian Doctrine of Grace* (New York: MacMillan, 1947), 9.

9. John Calvin, *Institutes of the Christian Religion*, ed. John T. McNeill, trans. Ford Lewis Battles, Library of Christian Classics (Philadelphia: Westminster Press, 1960), 537 (3.1.1).

10. Nikolaus Ludwig von Zinzendorf, "Jesus, Thy Blood and Righteousness," 1739, as quoted in C. H. Spurgeon, *All of Grace: An Earnest Word for Those Who Are Seeking Salvation by the Lord Jesus Christ* (Chicago: Moody Press, nd), 24.

11. Lewis B. Smedes, *Shame and Grace: Healing the Shame We Don't Deserve* (San Francisco: HarperSanFrancisco, 1993), 108.

Chapter Two: The Providence Mystery

1. John Flavel, *The Mystery of Providence* (Edinburgh: Banner of Truth, 1963), 15.

2. "The Orthodox Creed," in John Broadus, *Baptist Confessions, Covenants, and Catechisms*, ed. Timothy and Denise George (Nashville: Broadman and Holman, 1996), 101–2.

3. Robert A. Baker, ed., *A Baptist Source Book* (Nashville: Broadman Press, 1966), 138.

4. Dale Moody, *The Word of Truth* (Grand Rapids: Eerdmans, 1981), 137.

5. G. K. Chesterton, *Orthodoxy* (New York: John Lane Company, 1908), 174.

6. Wayne Grudem, *Systematic Theology* (Grand Rapids: Zondervan, 1994), 270–71.

7. G. C. Berkouwer, *The Providence of God* (Grand Rapids: Eerdmans, 1952), 151–52.

8. Ibid., 162.

9. William Cowper, "God Moves in a Mysterious Way," 1774.

10. Edward Mote, "The Solid Rock," 1834.

11. Carlyle Marney, *The Crucible of Redemption* (Wake Forest, NC: Chanticleer, 1968), 62.

12. Isaac Watts, "Begin, My Tongue, Some Heavenly Theme," 1707.

Chapter Three: Saved by Grace

1. J. I. Packer, *Evangelism and the Sovereignty of God* (London: Inter-Varsity Press, 1961), 17.

2. From Ella Wheeler Wilcox, "Will," in *Maurine and Other Poems* (Chicago: W. B. Conkey, 1888), 144.

3. William Ernest Henley, "Invictus," in *The Best Loved Poems of the American People*, ed. Hazel Felleman (New York: Garden City, 1936), 73.

4. James B. Taylor, *Memoir of Rev. Luther Rice: One of the First American Missionaries to the East* (Nashville: Broadman, 1841), 293–94.

5. Augustine, *The Confessions*, ed. John E. Rotelle, trans. Maria Boulding (Hyde Park, NY: New City Press, 1997), 62–63 (2.2, 2.4).

6. Ibid., 207 (8.29).

7. E. Gordon Rupp and Philip S. Watson, eds., *Luther and Erasmus: Free Will and Salvation*, Library of Christian Classics (Philadelphia: Westminster Press, 1969), 47.

8. Theodore G. Tappert, ed., *Luther: Letters of Spiritual Counsel*, Library of Christian Classics (Philadelphia: Westminster Press, 1955), 116.

9. John Calvin, *Institutes of the Christian Religion*, ed. John T. McNeill, trans. Ford Lewis Battles, Library of Christian Classics (Philadelphia: Westminster Press, 1960), 925 (3.21.4).

10. Arnold A. Dallimore, *George Whitefield: God's Anointed Servant in the Great Revival of the Eighteenth Century* (Westchester, IL: Crossway, 1990), 197.

11. Timothy George, *John Robinson and the English Separatist Tradition* (Macon, GA: Mercer University Press, 1982), 91.

12. Packer, *Evangelism and the Sovereignty of God*, 13–14.

Chapter Four: A Graceful Theology

1. Helmut Thielicke, *The Waiting Father* (San Francisco: Harper and Row, 1959), 133.

2. David Benedict, *A General History of the Baptist Denomination in America*, 2 vols. (Boston: Lincoln and Edmonds, 1813), 2:456.

3. Quoted in Thomas J. Nettles, *By His Grace and for His Glory* (Grand Rapids: Baker, 1986), 50.

4. Paige Patterson, "SBC President Patterson Expands on Various Points of Calvinism," *The Alabama Baptist*, December 2, 1999, 11.

5. Cornelius Plantinga Jr., *Not the Way It's Supposed to Be: A Breviary of Sin* (Grand Rapids: Eerdmans, 1995), 199.

6. "I Sought the Lord, and Afterward I Knew," (anonymous) ca. 1878.

7. Charles Haddon Spurgeon, *Metropolitan Tabernacle Pulpit*, 14:200.

8. Robert A. Baker, ed., *A Baptist Source Book* (Nashville: Broadman Press, 1966), 208.

9. J. I. Packer, *Concise Theology: A Guide to Historic Christian Beliefs* (Wheaton, IL: Tyndale, 1993), 149.

10. Spurgeon, *Metropolitan Tabernacle Pulpit*, 8:58.

11. Ibid., 17:449.

12. Ibid., 12:477.

13. Baptist Faith and Message.

14. Charles Wesley, "And Can It Be," 1738.

15. Nettles, *By His Grace and for His Glory*, 231.

16. Charles Haddon Spurgeon, *Sermons on Sovereignty* (Pasadena, TX: Pilgrim, 1990), 92.

17. Abraham Booth, *The Reign of Grace: Its Rise to Its Consummation* (Swengel, PA: Reiner, 1976), 48.

18. Quoted in Ernest Kevan, *Moral Law* (Phillipsburg, NJ: Presbyterian and Reformed, 1991), 74–75.

Chapter Five: Grace and the Great Commission

1. Oswald Chambers, *My Utmost for His Highest* (Westwood, NJ: Barbour, 1963), 195.

2. Robert A. Baker, *Baptist Source Book* (Nashville: Broadman Press, 1966), 209.

3. John Broadus, *Baptist Confessions, Covenants, and Catechisms*, ed. Timothy and Denise George (Nashville: Broadman and Holman, 1996), 70.

4. Iain H. Murray, *Spurgeon v. Hyper-Calvinism: The Battle for Gospel Preaching* (Edinburgh: Banner of Truth, 1995), 120.

5. Erdmann Neumeister, "Jesus nimnt die Sünder an" (1722), quoted in Gustav Warneck, *Outline of a History of Protestant Missions from the Reformation to the Present Time: A Contribution to Modern Church History* (New York: Revell, 1901), 57. Digitized by Google and available online.

6. Ernest A. Payne, *The Church Awakes* (London: Carey Press, 1942), 97.

7. Ibid., 56–57, summarizing Andrew Fuller, *The Gospel Worthy of All Acceptation* (Boston: American Doctrinal Tract Society, 1846), 23–80.

8. Nevill B. Cryer, "Biography of John Eliot," in *Five Pioneer Missionaries* (London: Banner of Truth, 1965), 221.

9. F. A. Cox, *History of the Baptist Missionary Society from 1792–1842*, 2 vols. (London: T. Ward and Co., 1842), 1:20:115.

10. Eustace Carey, *Memoir of William Carey, D.D.: Late Missionary to Bengal; Professor of Oriental Languages in the College of Fort William, Calcutta* (London: Jackson and Walford, 1836), 168. Digitized by Google and available online.

11. Ibid., 75.

12. Letter from Andrew Fuller to John Fawcett, Kettering (Yorkshire), England, August 30, 1793.

13. T. E. Holling, "Epitaphs," in *Methodist Magazine and Review: Devoted to Religion, Literature and Social Progress*, ed. W. H. Withrow, vol. 53, July–December, 1901 (Toronto: William Briggs, Methodist Publishing House, 1901), 157. Digitized by Google and available online.

14. Charles Haddon Spurgeon, *Metropolitan Tabernacle Pulpit*, 42:234.

15. Ibid., 30:630.

16. Lewis Drummond, *Spurgeon: Prince of Preachers* (Grand Rapids: Kregel, 1992), 301.

17. Ibid., 290.

18. Spurgeon, *Metropolitan Tabernacle Pulpit*, 30:54–55.

19. Quoted in Anthony A. Hoekema, *Saved by Grace* (Grand Rapids: Eerdmans, 1989), 105.

20. Murray, *Spurgeon v. Hyper-Calvinism*, 94.

21. Spurgeon, *Metropolitan Tabernacle Pulpit*, 32:580–81.

22. Quoted in Timothy George and David S. Dockery, eds., *Baptist Theologians* (Nashville: Broadman, 1990), 95.

23. Charles Haddon Spurgeon, *An All-Round Ministry: Addresses to Ministers and Students* (Edinburgh: Banner of Truth, 1986), 285.

24. Spurgeon, *Metropolitan Tabernacle Pulpit*, 52:101.

Chapter Six: Living by Grace

1. Charles Haddon Spurgeon, *Metropolitan Tabernacle Pulpit*, 48:274.

2. George Whitefield, *Journals* (Edinburgh: Banner of Truth, 1960), 46.

3. Augustus Toplady, "Rock of Ages," 1775.

4. Quoted in Lewis B. Smedes, *Shame and Grace: Healing the Shame We Don't Deserve* (San Francisco: HarperSanFrancisco, 1993), 111.

5. T. W. Hunt, *The Doctrine of Prayer* (Nashville: Convention Press, 1986), 8.

6. "Albania's Access to Gospel Attributed to Prayer," *The Alabama Baptist* October 14, 1999, 4.

7. Ibid.

8. Ibid.

9. John Wesley, *The Works of the Rev. John Wesley*, vol. 10 (London: Wesleyan Conference Office, 1872), 360–61.

10. Iain H. Murray, *The Forgotten Spurgeon* (London: Banner of Truth, 1966), 65.

11. Henry Drummond, *The Greatest Thing in the World* (Birmingham, AL: Samford University Press, 1997), 57–58.

12. Quoted in ibid., xiii.

13. John Charles Ryle, *Old Paths* (London: James Clarke & Co., 1972), 468.

14. Charles Wesley, "And Can It Be," 1738.

Scripture Index

Scripture Index